A KID'S GUIDE TO CATS

Arden Moore

Storey Publishing

The mission of Storey Publishing is to serve our customers by publishing practical information that encourages personal independence in harmony with the environment.

Edited by Deanna F. Cook and Lisa H. Hiley
Art direction and book design by Alethea Morrison
Text production by Liseann Karandisecky
Indexed by Nancy D. Wood

Cover photography by © Andrey Kuzmin/Alamy
Stock Photo, back; © Ekaterina Kolomeets/stock
.adobe.com, spine; © sonsedskaya/stock.adobe
.com, front; © Stegarau/iStock.com, front (eyes)
Interior photography by Mars Vilaubi
Additional photography credits on page 144
Craft styling by Liseann Karandisecky
Illustrations by © Ryan Wheatcroft

Storey Publishing
210 MASS MoCA Way
North Adams, MA 01247
storey.com

Printed in China through World Print
10 9 8 7 6 5 4 3

Storey books are available at special discounts when purchased in bulk for premiums and sales promotions as well as for fund-raising or educational use. Special editions or book excerpts can also be created to specification. For details, please call 800-827-8673, or send an email to sales@storey.com.

Library of Congress Cataloging-in-Publication Data

Names: Moore, Arden, author.
Title: A kid's guide to cats : how to train, care for, and play and communicate with your amazing pet! / Arden Moore.
Description: North Adams : Storey Publishing, 2020. | Includes index. | Audience: Ages 8–12 | Audience: Grades 2–3 | Summary: "This fun and practical cat care book written just for kids will guide young cat owners in how to take care of their feline friends"— Provided by publisher.
Identifiers: LCCN 2019041930 (print) | LCCN 2019041931 (ebook) | ISBN 9781635861013 (paperback) | ISBN 9781635861020 (hardcover) | ISBN 9781635861037 (ebook)
Subjects: LCSH: Cats—Juvenile literature. | Cats—Training—Juvenile literature.
Classification: LCC SF447 .M675 2020 (print) | LCC SF447 (ebook) | DDC 636.8—dc23
LC record available at https://lccn.loc .gov/2019041930
LC ebook record available at https://lccn.loc .gov/2019041931

I HONOR ALL THE CATS IN MY LIFE, PAST AND PRESENT, WHO HAVE TAUGHT ME MANY VALUABLE LIFE LESSONS.

Special appreciation goes to my "writing partner" for this book, my confident orange tabby, best known as Pet Safety Cat Casey.

A big paws-up also goes to my pet-loving family, especially Julie, Kevin, Karen, Rick, Deb, and Jill.

Contents

Hi, kids!

Arden and Casey

Cats are cool. You know it. I know it. And cats certainly know it!

Ever since I was eight years old, I've been fortunate to always have a cat or two in my life. My childhood cat, Corky, was a friendly, adventurous Siamese. He joined me each time I fished off the pier in our backyard lake in Crown Point, Indiana. He loved eating bluegill fish I caught. He also enjoyed swimming with our two dogs to the raft in the middle of our small lake. When we kids were done swimming, I would place Corky back in the water and he would happily paddle back to shore, using his long tail as a rudder. Once back on land, Corky shook each wet paw and found a sunny spot to finish grooming.

Since Corky, I've had cats named Samantha, Murphy, Callie, Little Guy (a.k.a. Dude), Zeki, Mikey, Mort, and

now Casey. Each one had a different purr-sonality, and each one made my life a bit better. And I know the special cat in your life does the same.

All cats deserve to feel safe, learn, and spend time with their favorite person — you! Casey and I are here to give you what you need to become your cat's best friend, whether you just got a new kitty or you have had a cat in the family for a long time. Time to unleash the learning and fun activities!

Paws up!

MEET CASEY

Your feline guide throughout this book is Pet Safety Cat Casey. He is a comical, confident orange tabby whom I adopted from the San Diego Humane Society when he was just four months old. This long, lean purring machine charms everyone he meets — and that includes other cats and dogs!

Casey also loves to learn. He has aced how to come on cue, sit, sit up, touch paws to say hello, and do a 360-degree slow spin. He walks nicely on a leash and sits tall and proud inside a pet stroller as I push it. He's even willing to sport a cowboy hat or a bow tie when required.

Casey is always game to explore new places. Together we have traveled to 12 states to give our pet first-aid classes and pet behavior talks. Locally, he visits kids at animal shelter critter camps and seniors at memory-care centers as a certified therapy cat. Look for Casey's tips throughout the pages of this book, as he has a lot of good things to meow about!

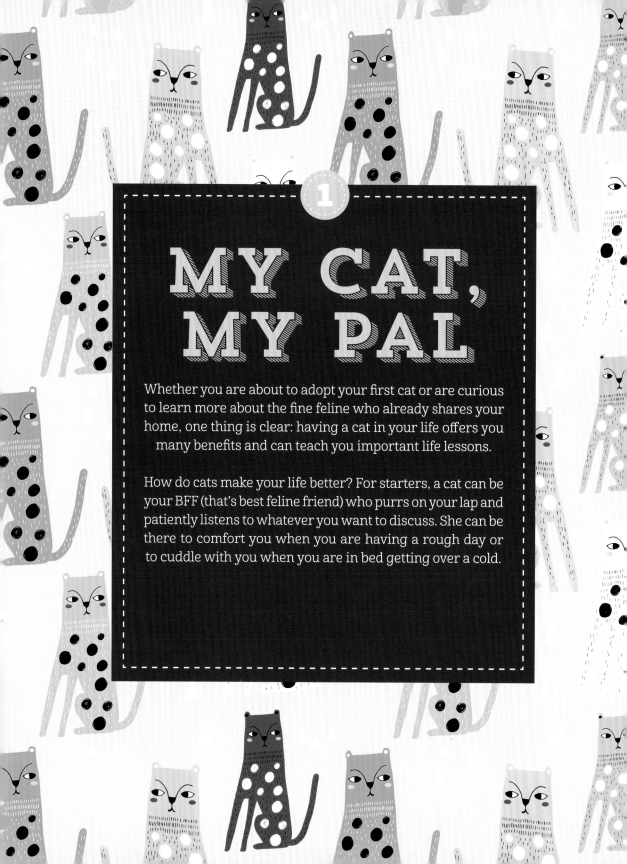

MY CAT, MY PAL

Whether you are about to adopt your first cat or are curious to learn more about the fine feline who already shares your home, one thing is clear: having a cat in your life offers you many benefits and can teach you important life lessons.

How do cats make your life better? For starters, a cat can be your BFF (that's best feline friend) who purrs on your lap and patiently listens to whatever you want to discuss. She can be there to comfort you when you are having a rough day or to cuddle with you when you are in bed getting over a cold.

Have you heard the saying "Laughter is the best medicine"? A cat can make you laugh out loud, especially when she is zooming around the house or playing inside an empty box or waiting in the bathtub for you to turn on the faucet so it goes drip-drip-drip. It's hard to feel sad or lonely when you have a cat to amuse and entertain you.

A cat can also teach you an important skill: patience. Because cats tend to be solitary in nature and many are somewhat shy, you'll learn to wait and chill out until your kitty is ready to play. You'll learn to approach her slowly and speak in a calm voice, so she'll want to hang out rather than dash from the room because you've startled her. Learning to zero in on her feelings and needs is good practice for being thoughtful of others, too.

Count on your cat to teach you responsibility as well. After all, your feline pal is counting on you to feed her, groom her, play with her, and, yes, keep her litter box clean.

CATS ARE GOOD FOR YOUR HEALTH!

Here are three major health benefits of having a cat in your life:

* Cats reduce stress and anxiety. Nervous about a big math test? Turn to your purring four-legger. A petting session with your cat can release calming brain chemicals, lower blood pressure, and slow your heart rate. Pretty cool!

* You may suffer fewer allergies (achoo!). Kids exposed to cats at a young age are less likely to develop various allergies, including to dust mites, ragweed, and grass.

* Purring is one of the most comforting, soothing sounds in the world. The sound has even been known to help people with joint injuries.

It's Purr-fect!

I love to purr when I'm content. Here's a cool feline fact: many big cats, like pumas, also purr, but big cats that roar, like lions, don't purr. We cats can purr continuously as we inhale and exhale. I bet you can't do that! Try it — you will only be able to purr while exhaling.

purrs

Roars and cannot purr

purrs

11

LET YOUR CAT BE A CAT

One of the best gifts you can give your cat is to not treat him like a little person or a funny-looking dog. Cats think, act, and behave differently than humans and dogs. It's important to treat your cat like the fine, furry feline he is!

Unlike dogs, cats are not born pleasers. Here are five other important differences between cats and dogs.

1 Cats are solitary hunters and, while they are social, they don't need other pets or people to feel content. Dogs hunt in packs and usually feel happier with company.

2 Cats tend to be more active at dawn and dusk (this is called being crepuscular). Dogs are more active during the day (diurnal).

3 Even affectionate cats typically prefer to stay behind when you leave the house. Most dogs like to be wherever their favorite people are and don't mind exploring new places.

4 The vast majority of cats instinctively know how to use a litter box once you show them where it is (and as long as you keep it clean). Dogs need lots of help to develop their house-training skills.

5 Cats make a wide variety of sounds (up to 100, according to some research!), while dogs have a more limited "vocabulary" of about 20 sounds. But dogs have a much larger range of facial expressions.

Ricky, mighty bubble hunter

CATS RULE, DOGS DROOL

Candid   **D**rool

Attitude   **O**bey

Tenacious   **G**oofy

So what?   **S**econds, please!

A VERY BRIEF
HISS-TORY LESSON

Cats have had a love/loathe relationship with people for centuries. Cats are very patient and are masters at observing what goes on around them. That may explain in part why they waited about ten thousand years after dogs were domesticated to enter into a partnership with people. First domesticated about nine thousand years ago in Egypt, cats were worshipped as gods. But in Europe in the Middle Ages, cats were falsely linked to witchcraft and superstition, and thousands of them were killed.

Fortunately, cats eventually made their way back into humans' good graces. A big reason is that wherever people stored grain and foodstuffs, they needed cats to keep rodents at bay. For example, cats were important crew members aboard ships that explored the world — without cats, rats and mice would have eaten much of the sailors' food. Today, cats are among the most beloved and popular of pets. In fact, cats outnumber dogs in American households by 86 million to 78 million. Many are Instagram stars with millions of faithful followers. Sorry, Fido!

Ancient Egyptians believed that the cat goddess Bastet protected the Pharaohs.

Since the Middle Ages, cats have been associated with witchcraft and superstition.

Cat Speak!

Kids and cats are friends all over the world. Impress *your* friends by learning how to say "cat" in these languages:

Arabic
qetta (KU-tah)

Cherokee
wesa (WAY-sah)

French
chat (sha)

German
Katze (KAT-suh)

Hebrew
*cha'tool
(kha-TOOL)*

Hawaiian
*popoki
(poe-poe-kee)*

Russian
*koshka
(kush-kah)*

**Thai/
Vietnamese**
meo (maow)

Italian
gatto (GAH-toe)

Spanish
gato (GAH-toe)

15

NICE TO MEET YOU, MS. KITTY

Even though cats have been domesticated for the past nine thousand years or so, many are cautious and a bit wary when first meeting someone. They are not going to gallop up like a goofy dog to say hello and accept you as a friend the first time you meet.

To successfully greet a cat at a shelter or at a friend's house, you need to honor the cardinal rule of feline introductions: let the cat make the first move. Even if you pride yourself as being a friendly, outgoing person,

restrain yourself. Felines, whether they are outgoing or shy, prefer meeting people on their terms. That means no forced introductions. No wild gestures. No loud voices. No stare-downs. Any or all of these actions are apt to make the cat dash out of the room and into hiding.

TAKE IT SLOWLY

If the cat seems curious but is still a bit standoffish, try winning her over with treats or toys. Gently toss a treat

Stranger danger!

Signs to Watch For

When you're meeting a new cat, pay attention to her body language. Some cats prefer less handling and attention than others. A fearful cat is apt to bring her feet closer to her body and lower her head to make herself appear smaller. Her back will arch and her ears will flatten when you approach — all signals that she feels threatened and may either flee or take a swat at you. If you ignore these cues and move closer, she may hiss, a warning to stay away.

But if the cat displays soft eyes, upright ears, upright tail, and relaxed body, she is indicating that she feels comfortable with you.

or two away from you so she can eat without fear of being caught. Or try tossing a small cat toy for her to chase. Some cats are happy to play but would rather not be petted.

Cats vary in temperament and social skills. While some confidently greet new people and are happy to make friends, most take their sweet time to warm up to a stranger. By playing a little hard to get and allowing them to make the first move in the introduction, you will have a better chance at creating long-lasting friendships built on trust. Turn the page to learn my recommended approach for winning over a kitty who is timid or shy.

CASEY'S COMMENT

Blink Softly, Please

I'm going to let a cat-greeting secret out of the bag. One great way to deliver a kitty hello is to slowly blink your eyes at the cat. Then wait and watch for her reaction. A welcoming cat will respond by softly winking back at you and may even start purring. When I do this with my favorite people, I often earn a tasty treat. Sweet!

GREETING A NEW CAT

1 **Move slowly and quietly, keeping your hands still.** Use a soft voice and don't look directly at the cat — staring can be interpreted as a threat by a wary feline. In fact, hard as it might be, just ignore the cat completely.

2 **Sit down and let the cat approach you.** Cats are curious by nature, so give her a chance to check you out. Breathe slowly and calmly to show that you aren't going to make a sudden move. Cats can sniff out your emotional state and sense if you are feeling happy, sad, nervous, or angry.

3 **As the cat approaches you, continue to avoid eye contact.** Expect some "one step forward, two steps back" action as she checks you out.

4 When the cat is ready, let her make the first move. A cat may touch her nose against your leg, sniff your shoe, or boldly rub her body against you. Keep breathing calmly and sitting still. You can take a quick look at the cat and slowly look away.

5 Extend your index finger to the cat's head. Felines all over the world will recognize this as an invitation to rub their cheek on your finger, the feline equivalent of a handshake. Allow the cat to sniff your finger. She may turn her head and allow your finger to glide across her cheek. Or she may lower her head and bump against you.

6 Move your finger lightly down her back. If she likes that, stroke with your whole hand, moving from head to tail. Gently see if she is ready to accept a soft ear rub or an under-the-chin scratch. Always watch how she behaves and be ready to stop touching her.

THINK LIKE A CAT

Time for a lesson in cat-titude, or what's going on in that feline mind.

PREDATOR AND PREY. You probably know that cats are predators, meaning they will hunt and kill smaller animals, but did you know that they can also be preyed upon themselves? This puts them an unusual position in the animal world. They can be fierce hunters, but they are always on alert for danger from a larger predator, like a coyote or a big hawk.

NOT SO ALOOF. Even though cats have a reputation for being standoffish and unsocial, most of them do like to be around familiar people and will happily share a home with other animals. It's true that they are more independent than dogs and don't mind spending time alone. That doesn't mean they can fend for themselves while you go on vacation, however! They still need attention and companionship.

CASEY'S COMMENT

We Know What We Like

People like to say that cats are finicky, but I disagree. It's true that we're more selective about what we eat than canine chowhounds. Perhaps one reason is that cats have only 473 taste buds (dogs have 1,700!), so we like food that has a lot of flavor, which usually means it smells strongly, too, like fish. Yum!

YAWN AND STRETCH. Although they like to play and prowl around, cats don't expend a lot of energy. Just like many kids, they love to sleep, and they hate to be woken up. In fact, most cats sleep as much as 16 to 18 hours a day! (Where do you think the word *catnap* came from?)

NO SURPRISES. Cats are creatures of habit who crave routines. They like to know what to expect and when to expect it. For example, even though they don't wear watches, they know when it is mealtime and when you should come home from school, and they'll be waiting.

DECODING CAT CHAT

In cat-to-cat interactions, the "conversation" is usually dominated by silence and body posture. But when it comes to cats and people, our feline friends have learned to speak up more. Cats are quick studies. They realize that we humans are often oblivious to the body language that is obvious to other cats. So they have learned to make a range of different sounds with different meanings that they use only to communicate with people. Pretty smart, huh?

CATS ARE STRAIGHT TALKERS. They never deceive or pretend. If they feel threatened or angered, they hiss or growl or seek an escape route. If they feel content, they may purr or mew in a soft, friendly way. And don't be fooled for a minute that cats don't know key words like *treat* and *dinner* and commands like "Hey, get off the table!"

Here are some common cat sounds and what they mean.

CHIRP. This musical trill comes from the throat and sounds almost like a question. Directed at a favorite person, this sound conveys "I'm glad you are here" or "Oh, there you are."

MEW. This pleasant, high-pitched sound is used to prompt people to do a cat's bidding, as in "Please refill the food bowl" or "Scratch under my chin."

MEOW. This drawn-out, urgent-sounding tone is employed by a cat who has demands and is displeased. The cat is telling you that you forgot to feed him or he wants to go outside.

I love you the very most.

PURR. Most of the time, cats make this rumbling noise in their throats when they are content. A mother cat purrs when nursing her kittens, so it is a comforting sound to her litter. However, cats also purr when they are scared, so don't be surprised if your cat revs up at the veterinary clinic.

24

CACKLE. Your cat may make this chattering *ka-ka-ka* sound when he spots a bird or squirrel through the window. It means he is both excited at the sight of potential prey and frustrated that he can't reach it. Don't pet him when he is doing this; if you startle him, he may respond by swatting or biting.

HISS. This angry sound is easy to interpret. The cat is telling you to back off. An especially furious or frightened cat will make a spitting sound as well.

HISSs

GROWL. A very angry cat will make it clear, usually to another cat, that a fight is brewing if someone doesn't back down and back off. Or he may deliver a low growl while protecting a favorite toy or to indicate he does *not* wish to be petted or picked up. Heed this warning or the cat may bring out the claws.

Go ahead.
I dare you.

It's Bonk Time!

When I really like someone, I gently lower my head and bump it against that person's forehead — bonk! This is a feline way to show a special person deep affection. We're marking that person with our scent to show that he or she belongs to our inner friendship circle. Cats who do this usually rev up the purring volume, too.

YOWL. This drawn-out screech is only heard from a cat who is furious or in serious pain. It's most often heard during an outdoor fight between rivals. If your cat yowls when you touch him, he needs to see his veterinarian.

TRIVIA
QUIZ 1

1. True or false: Cats can see in total darkness.

2. True or false: All kittens are born with blue eyes.

3. True or false: Cats only purr when they are content.

4. True or False: There's a breed of cat nicknamed the Swimming Cat.

See page 138 for the answers.

GUESS MY MOOD

Just like you, your cat can display a wide range of moods, from happy to sad to scared to angry. It can be tricky trying to figure out what mood your cat is in. So, let's play pet detective and hunt for telltale clues.

Tensing muscles and flattening ears. If you also notice twitching skin and some unhappy growling or yowling, this is a cat who feels threatened, perhaps by another cat or an overly enthusiastic dog. Or she may be in pain due to an injury or a medical issue. Don't try to pet or pick up your cat in this mood. If you think she's hurt, tell your parents.

Purring and rubbing against your leg. This is a relaxed, happy cat seeking your affection. She may also deliver soft-eyed winks and attempt to jump in your lap.

Flopping over in a relaxed manner. Here's a cat who feels secure around you and is signaling that she wants attention. Stick to petting her head and ears — not her belly — until you build up trust. Some cats do not like their bellies rubbed.

Racing around with wide eyes. This cat in is play mode. She is looking for ways to burn off pent-up energy and use her brain. Join in the fun by tossing a toy mouse for her to chase or waving a feather wand for her to pursue.

Toys! I need TOYS!

KEEP AN EYE ON THE EARS AND TAIL

Cats convey a lot about their moods by the position of their ears and the action of their tails.

A friendly, trusting cat has upright, relaxed ears. He hoists his tail in the air as he greets his favorite people.

A curious cat perks his ears forward and may twitch the end of his tail.

A frightened cat flattens his ears to the side and puffs his tail to appear larger.

An angry or threatened cat pins his ears back and lashes his tail back and forth.

BODY BY CAT

RETRACTABLE CLAWS come out to catch prey and grip surfaces. There are 5 claws on each front paw and 4 on each back paw, for a total of 18.

COATS come in short, medium, and long lengths and myriad colors and patterns. Coats are designed to protect cats from weather extremes.

FLEXIBLE SPINE aids in running, leaping, jumping, and landing on the feet.

TAIL acts as a rudder when running, climbing, or swimming, and is also a mood barometer.

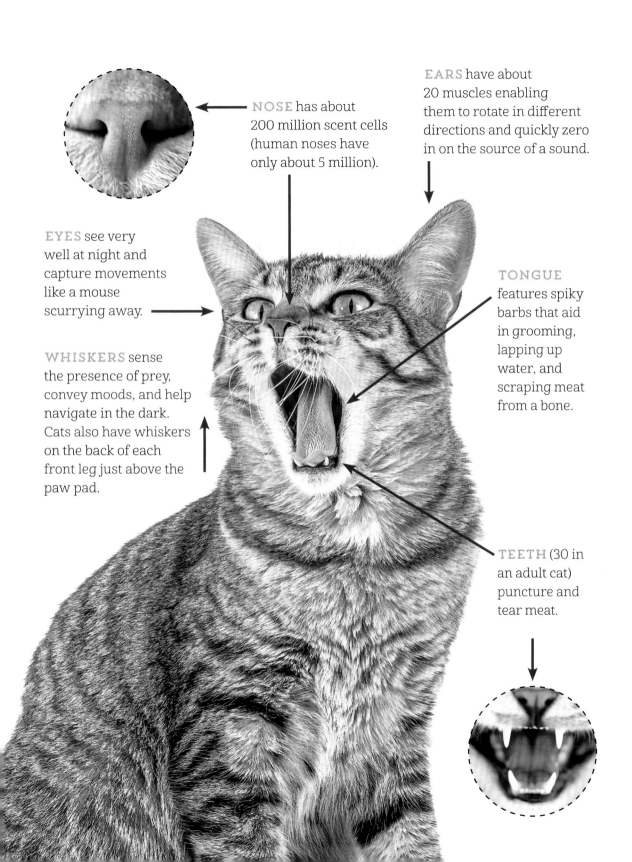

NOSE has about 200 million scent cells (human noses have only about 5 million).

EARS have about 20 muscles enabling them to rotate in different directions and quickly zero in on the source of a sound.

EYES see very well at night and capture movements like a mouse scurrying away.

TONGUE features spiky barbs that aid in grooming, lapping up water, and scraping meat from a bone.

WHISKERS sense the presence of prey, convey moods, and help navigate in the dark. Cats also have whiskers on the back of each front leg just above the paw pad.

TEETH (30 in an adult cat) puncture and tear meat.

SOME POPULAR CAT BREEDS

There are about three times as many dog breeds than cat breeds because dogs have been bred over centuries to do specific jobs. Most cats aren't any particular breed, but quite a few special breeds of cats have been developed, mostly for their looks. If you plan to adopt a purebred cat or want to know something cool about the one you have, read on!

MAINE COON. This gentle giant can weigh up to 18 pounds, but despite its size, this breed emits sweet chirps. The Maine coon puts the *m* in mellow and tends to get along with people, other cats, and even dogs.

Maine coons have furry paws, long fluffy tails, and tufts of hair on their ears (check out the opposite page).

PERSIAN. With its flat face, expressive round eyes, and long, flowing coat, the Persian has reigned as one of the most popular cat breeds in North America since it appeared at the first known cat show in 1871 in London.

Persians tend to be sweet and smart and are not big talkers.

ABYSSINIAN. With jungle looks and green or gold almond-shaped eyes, the Abyssinian is nicknamed the "bunny cat" for its soft, rabbitlike coat. This smart, acrobatic cat needs lots of attention and regular play sessions to keep out of mischief.

Abys, as they're called, like being around people but aren't much for sitting on laps.

SIAMESE. The Siamese has a long,
lean body with a triangular-shaped
head and huge blue eyes. This outgoing,
adventure-seeking feline is a chatty cat
who often sounds like a human baby.

RAGDOLL. A relatively new breed that originated in California in the 1960s, the Ragdoll is a people-loving cat who often goes limp when picked up, as the name implies. This large breed (males can weigh up to 20 pounds) has a reputation for being gentle and polite, even around kids.

SPHYNX. The hairless Sphynx looks a bit like a friendly space alien with large eyes, huge ears, wrinkled skin, and a long, skinny tail. These cats love to play and snuggle under the covers to stay warm.

JUST A REGULAR CAT, THANK YOU

Most cats don't have purebred pedigrees like the fancy breeds described in the previous pages. They are identified on their papers at the rescue shelter or veterinarian's office as "domestic short hair" (DSH) or "domestic long hair" (DLH), depending on the length of their coats. These cats come in a huge range of colors and markings. Topping the list of popular cat colors are calicos, tortoiseshells, tuxedo cats, and orange tabbies, all of which can have short or long or in-between coats. Here's a little bit of information about each one.

calico

CALICO CATS are tricolored, often with patches of color on white.

TORTOISESHELL CATS, or torties, have two or more colors without any white. They are generally female and have a reputation for being a bit feisty and independent. They tend to prefer a quiet household with a set routine.

Tortoiseshell calico

TUXEDO CATS are mostly black with a white chest, face, and paws. Some have lots of white, some just a little. There are many other combinations of black and white fur, but tuxedo cats look like they are dressed up for a fancy party. Some even sport a bow tie or mustache with their suit! Many tuxedo lovers claim that these cats are friendly and laid back.

Tuxedo

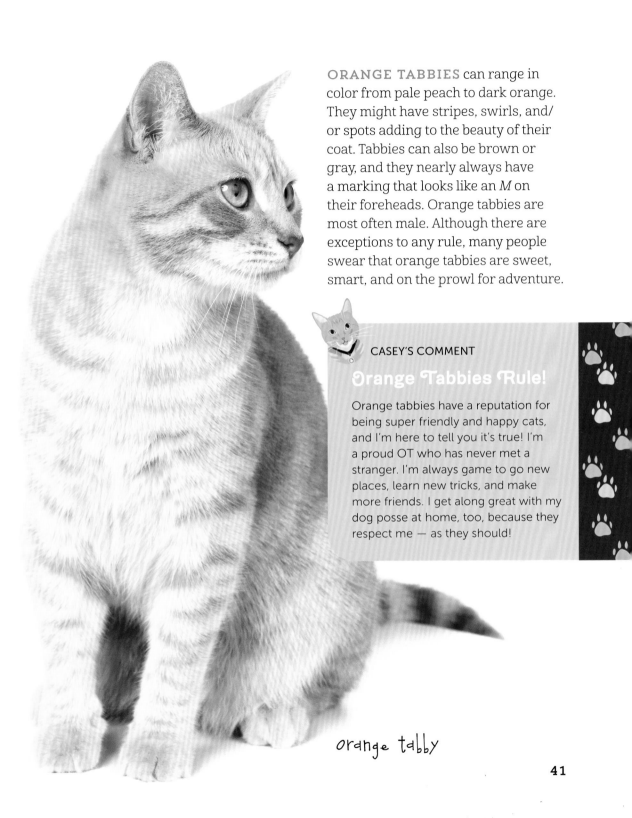

ORANGE TABBIES can range in color from pale peach to dark orange. They might have stripes, swirls, and/or spots adding to the beauty of their coat. Tabbies can also be brown or gray, and they nearly always have a marking that looks like an *M* on their foreheads. Orange tabbies are most often male. Although there are exceptions to any rule, many people swear that orange tabbies are sweet, smart, and on the prowl for adventure.

CASEY'S COMMENT

Orange Tabbies Rule!

Orange tabbies have a reputation for being super friendly and happy cats, and I'm here to tell you it's true! I'm a proud OT who has never met a stranger. I'm always game to go new places, learn new tricks, and make more friends. I get along great with my dog posse at home, too, because they respect me — as they should!

orange tabby

ADOPTION DEBATE: KITTEN OR CAT?

Should you adopt a young kitten or an adult or even a senior cat? If you already have a cat or two (or more!) in your household, you've probably had this debate. Maybe you're thinking of adding another cat to your family or you are ready for your first feline pet. Each choice brings pluses and challenges. Before you and your family decide, think carefully through the following points. Chances are this feline will be with you for many years to come.

KITTEN (UNDER 1 YEAR OLD). Kittens are adorable and tons of fun, but keep in mind that they are babies and haven't learned how to be a good cat. Kittens are full of energy and curiosity and can be quite a handful during the first year. And they grow fast, usually reaching about 95 percent of their adult size by their first birthday. By socializing and training a kitten, you play a big role in her development and personality, but certain traits are inborn. A shy, quiet kitten will most likely grow into a shy, quiet cat.

Kittens are adorable but mischievous.

ADULT CAT (1 TO 12 YEARS OLD). With this age group, there should be no surprises in terms of the personality, likes, and dislikes. Generally, adult cats in their prime years are more mellow than kittens but are still up for play sessions with you. An older cat may be more accepting of the bustle of a busy household and may even know how to deal with dogs. If you adopt from a shelter, the staff will help you choose a good feline companion for your family.

SENIOR CAT (12 YEARS OR OLDER). Some cats live past 20 years. If your family opts to adopt a senior cat, you can still have many years to enjoy her company. Many older cats adapt well to a new home and often seem happy to have a second chance with a new family. Sure, some older cats may have health issues like arthritis, but they may still enjoy chasing a toy down the hall or batting around a catnip mouse.

Whatever age cat you choose, have any new pet checked by your vet. Kittens need a series of shots in their first year and should be spayed or neutered as well. Older cats also need certain shots and should have an overall exam that includes checking their teeth.

Adult cats are more mellow but are still up for play.

HOW OLD IS
YOUR CAT, REALLY?

It can be tricky to figure out the age of a cat. Unlike dogs, cats don't go gray in the muzzle when they become seniors. Veterinarians consider a 1-year-old cat to be about the same as a 15-year-old person.

That means by the time your cat celebrates her first birthday, she is halfway through being a teenager!

Check out this chart to get a rough idea of your cat's age in human terms.

 age of cat   human equivalent

age of cat	human equivalent	age of cat	human equivalent
1	15	8	48
2	24	9	52
3	28	10	56
4	32	11	60
5	36	12	64
6	40	13	68
7	44	14	72

 2 months

15 = 76   19 = 92

16 = 80   20 = 96

17 = 84

18 = 88

2 years

7 months

LIVING WITH A KITTEN

Welcome to the "wonder year." This is the best term to describe your first year living with a kitten. Why? Because with all that high energy and mischief-making in your house, you may wonder where your sanity has gone. Fast-growing kittens are full of energy, ready to explore, and constantly hungry. They need to play a lot and sleep a lot, not always when it's convenient for you! You'll have to be patient while your kitten figures out the difference between day and night.

Like any youngsters, kittens need to learn manners and household rules. Don't expect your kitten to immediately come when you call him or to sleep with you soundly all night. But that's okay. This is the ideal age to introduce some cool tricks to your kitten (see pages 97–107). You can also condition him to having his teeth brushed and nails clipped. Introduce a grooming routine early so by the time he is an adult, he will (hopefully) accept being cared for from his nails to his teeth!

A kitten needs special kitten food, not adult cat food, to grow properly. On average, a kitten puts on weight rapidly until about seven months of age, then gains steadily until his first birthday. It's okay if your young kitten looks slender, but he should not be bony or have a potbelly — these situations warrant a trip to the veterinarian clinic.

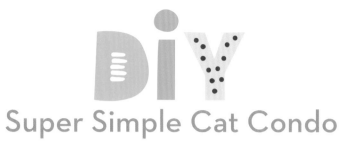

Super Simple Cat Condo

Cats love having a cozy spot to curl up in. See what your cat thinks of this easy-to-make hidey-hole.

A cardboard box just big enough for your cat to fit into

An old T-shirt large enough to cover the box

1 Tuck in or cut off the top flaps of the box to create one open side.

2 Slip the T-shirt over the box, with the neck over the open side.

3 Tuck in the sleeves on the sides and tie the bottom of the shirt in a knot opposite the neck opening. (Use string if necessary.)

4 Pop in a small pillow or folded towel to make a cozy cubbyhole for your kitty.

Most cats can't resist exploring an opening!

DiY
Creative Cat Castle

Use your imagination to make a multilevel space with several openings for hiding and playing.

Several boxes of different sizes

Scissors or box cutter

Glue

Fabric scraps, beads, cat toys, or other fun things to play with

Scratching post (optional)

You can use just one box, but cats love having different levels to play in, so it's more fun to use several. Figure out how you want to put them together, then cut a few holes in each box. Make some holes big enough for your cat to fit through and some just large enough for an exploring paw.

Glue the boxes together and let dry before decorating your creation with fabric strips and dangly toys. You can get really fancy and add a scratching post like the one shown on the opposite page (it's made of a mailing tube wrapped with burlap).

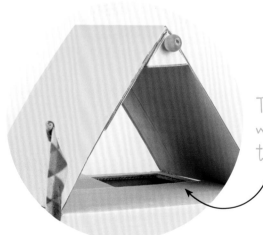

Try adding an attic with an entrance through the roof!

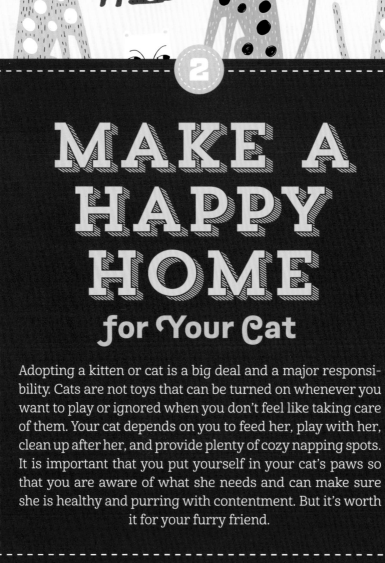

MAKE A HAPPY HOME
for Your Cat

Adopting a kitten or cat is a big deal and a major responsibility. Cats are not toys that can be turned on whenever you want to play or ignored when you don't feel like taking care of them. Your cat depends on you to feed her, play with her, clean up after her, and provide plenty of cozy napping spots. It is important that you put yourself in your cat's paws so that you are aware of what she needs and can make sure she is healthy and purring with contentment. But it's worth it for your furry friend.

INDOOR OR OUTDOOR?

Every family has to make a major decision about their cat: Will he live strictly indoors or be able to go outside, either under supervision or whenever he wants? There are a lot of factors to consider here. For an adult cat, for instance, your decision may depend on the cat and his history before you adopted him. The ultimate goal is to give your cat a safe and healthy life while making sure he is active and fulfilled. Check out the pros and cons in The Indoor/Outdoor Argument on page 54 and discuss your family's situation with your veterinarian.

My best solution for this debate? Keep your cat mostly inside and treat him to some cool cat furniture in the house, but also provide safe, supervised access to the great outdoors.

THE INDOOR/OUTDOOR ARGUMENT

INDOOR CATS

PROS

Typically live a longer, healthier life.

Incur fewer veterinary bills from fights, accidents, or illness.

Are safe from nibbling toxic garden plants or lapping up something poisonous, like car antifreeze.

May be more bonded to you because you spend more time together.

CONS

Can become bored and destructive if not provided with outlets for play and exercise.

May yowl a lot or always be looking for an open door to dart through.

With less exercise, may become chubby if meals aren't measured.

OUTDOOR CATS

PROS

Get plenty of exercise by unleashing their inner hunter.

Can climb trees and enjoy the sun without a harness or leash.

CONS

Risk being hit by cars, chased by dogs, or eaten by predators.

Risk getting lost and not being able to find their way home.

Will probably kill birds and other small animals — bad for the birds and exposes cats to parasites and disease.

More likely to pick up ticks and fleas.

ASK THE VET

What plants are dangerous to cats?

— Brilynn, age 12,
   The Woodlands, Texas

Sadly, I have had to treat hundreds of cases of poisoned pets, and many times, these cases were preventable if pet owners had realized that certain plants they have around their homes are toxic to their cats. Topping the list are lilies, especially Easter lilies. They are potentially fatal to cats if cats lick the pollen on their paws or nibble on just a couple of leaves.

Some other common houseplants that are toxic to cats are azaleas, chrysanthemums, English ivy, geraniums, oleander, and tulips. For a complete list, visit the ASPCA online.

If your cat is having trouble breathing, is drooling or vomiting, or has a rapid heartbeat, make sure your parents call ahead and take your cat to the nearest veterinary clinic, as this is a medical emergency.

— Dr. Michael LoSasso,
   Frisco Emergency Pet Care,
   Frisco, Texas

INDOOR ACCESSORIES

An indoor cat needs to claim some space for her own. It isn't difficult to provide a few spots where she can feel secure, take a nap, or get some exercise.

PICK A WINDOW WITH A GOOD VIEW and install a window perch where your cat can catch all the action going on outside. If you have bird feeders in sight, your cat will have her own TV channel to watch.

OFFER YOUR CAT A CARPETED CAT TREE or module unit that allows her to perch up high, move in and out, scratch, nap, and swat dangling toys. It's like a feline jungle gym!

PROVIDE A HIDEY-HOLE — a small space she can slip into for a catnap or to get away from too much attention (especially if you have an overly energetic dog). You can buy ready-made retreats called cat cubes or make one out of an old cabinet or sturdy cardboard box (see page 48).

IF YOU HAVE FLOOR-TO-CEILING POSTS in your basement or rec room, you can wrap them in thick sisal rope and invite your cat to hone her up-and-down climbing skills on this indoor "tree."

A FELINE WALL HIGHWAY ALLOWS CATS TO MOVE around a room from up high, their favorite angle. Your parents might agree to install an eye-catching catwalk made of shelving. Ideally, these catwalks should be about two feet wide to give your cat plenty of room to roam. Remember to look up — your cat may be prowling above you!

Is the coast clear yet?

Let's See Some ID

Even though I am an indoor cat, if someone forgets to close the front door, curiosity can lead me outside. Arden is pretty vigilant about keeping me safe. She had me microchipped at the vet's office. It was a quick and painless procedure to insert a chip about the size of a grain of rice between my shoulders. The chip contains contact info for my vet and for Arden. She also bought me a breakaway cat collar with my name and her cell phone number embroidered in bright orange. I look spiffy, and everybody knows my name!

A cat tree is like a feline jungle gym!

SAFE OUTDOOR OPTIONS

If you don't have an enclosed patio or screened-in porch where your cat can enjoy fresh air, consider creating an outdoor enclosure where your cat can hang out while your family is playing or gardening. It can be as simple as a large dog crate or as fancy as a converted chicken coop — there are lots of designs online. Always have a harness on your cat when moving him from the house to the enclosure so that he doesn't shoot away from you, and never leave him outside unsupervised.

A "CATIO" IS A FELINE-FINE ADDITION to consider. This is an enclosed space attached to your house that your cat can access from a window or special opening. Your cat can bask in sunlight and watch the world go by while being protected from predators and other hazards. It can be as simple or elaborate as your family's budget and skills allow.

IF YOU HAVE A BALCONY, make sure your cat is never out there unsupervised. Even if you're with him, he should wear a harness and be tethered to a leash. You don't want him to jump or fall and get injured. Ask your parents about screening in the balcony or installing a weatherproof safety net to protect your cat while he enjoys some fresh air.

Another option is to train your cat to wear a harness and walk on a leash so that you can take him for a walk in your backyard or down the street (see page 60). Or you can train your cat to ride in a pet stroller (see page 108).

CASEY'S COMMENT

I Love My Portable Tent

My feline brother, Mikey, and I are indoor cats. We used to sit in the window and meow in protest watching our three canine siblings romp and play outside on a sunny day. So, Arden bought us a cat tent that is totally enclosed with mesh windows and a zippered door. We love hanging out on the deck, feeling the breeze, sniffing the smells, and safely being part of the family's outdoor time.

WALK THIS WAY, KITTY!

Not all cats are candidates for walking on a leash, but it's worth trying if you have a curious and confident kitty. The process is easier with a kitten, but if you're patient, you might be surprised at the result. Use a properly fitted cat harness, with the leash attached to the D ring. Never use a collar for walking a cat because most cat collars are breakaway types, plus you don't want to risk injuring your cat's neck.

Spark your cat's interest by leaving the leash and harness in a place he'll see it often, like next to his favorite napping spot or by his food bowl. Once

or twice a day, offer him the leash and harness and reward him with a treat when he sniffs or paws at them. Drag the leash across the floor for your cat to pounce on. You want to build up a positive association with the leash. Do this for a few days until he's used to these new items.

When your cat is in a calm, relaxed mood, drape the harness over his body. Give him a treat. Let him get used to the feel of a harness on his body. Practice this over a few days before trying to put the harness on him, fitting it loosely at first. Move slowly

and don't force him. If he fusses, calmly remove it and go back to just draping it on him. Eventually, you should be able to adjust the harness to fit snugly, but not too tight — you should be able to fit a finger between his body and the straps.

Let him get comfortable wearing the harness around the house (with you giving plenty of treats), then step it up by attaching the leash and letting him drag it around (more treats!). After a few days, have another person hold the end of the leash while you entice your cat to come to you for a treat. This helps him get used to the feeling of the leash over his body instead of on the ground.

After your cat accepts leash-walking in the house, try an enclosed area outside like a fenced-in backyard or back porch. Keep your first outings to a minute or two and slowly build up the time as he becomes used to being outdoors. Be alert for dogs or cars going by, or other scary things.

Be patient and accept that leash-walking cats are not little dogs. Most cats who do accept being leashed prefer to decide when to walk, how fast, and in what direction. Let him sniff around or just lie down in the grass, if that's what he chooses to do.

Not all cats will take to walking on a leash, but it's a fun option if you have the patience to try it.

SIGN UP FOR CAT DUTY

Getting a kitten or cat can be an exciting time for your family. Everybody wants to play with the new family member, but it's important to create a daily pet chore schedule so that everybody takes care of her as well. If you already have a cat and no one is really in charge of taking care of her daily needs, it's time to step up and take on that responsibility.

If possible, have everyone in the home sign up for a cat job. Post a weekly or monthly calendar where everyone can see it — like on the refrigerator or a wall in the kitchen. Check off tasks as you complete them, so you don't accidently forget to do something. Then stand back and give yourself a pat on the back for a job well done. You are making life "meowvalous" for your feline friend.

CHOW TIME: Measure out the correct portion of kibble and/or wet food. You don't want to overfeed your BFF and cause her to become chubby.

WATER BOWL: Cats don't drink as much water as dogs do, but they need to stay hydrated. Empty and refill the bowl with fresh water every day.

LITTER BOX: See Litter Box Protocol on page 64.

PLAYTIME: Spend at least 10 to 15 minutes of one-on-one time with your kitty. Practice a new trick, cuddle with her, read to her, or engage her in a game of stalking a feather-wand toy.

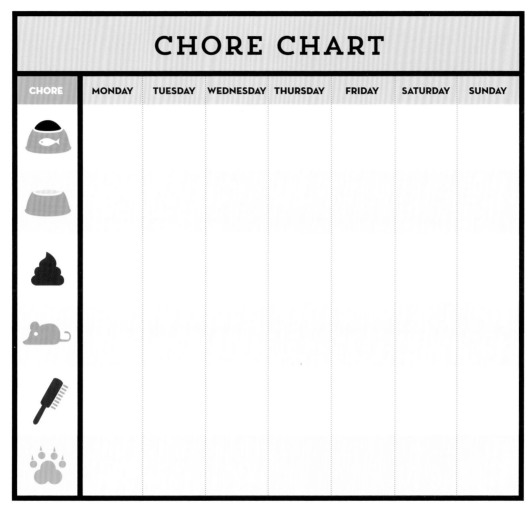

CHORE CHART

CHORE	MONDAY	TUESDAY	WEDNESDAY	THURSDAY	FRIDAY	SATURDAY	SUNDAY

Download and print the chore chart at www.storey.com/cat-chore-chart/

GROOMING: Depending on the hair coat of your cat, you may need to comb or brush her daily, a few times a week, or weekly. Do not let your cat's coat become matted. Mats are painful and can frustrate cats who are proud of their grooming skills.

NAIL CLIPPING: About once a month, inspect the length and condition of your cat's claws by gently pressing on each paw pad to reveal the claws. See page 120 for more on how to trim nails.

LITTER BOX PROTOCOL

We can all agree that cleaning your cat's "bathroom" ranks low on any list of fun things to do. But cats are fastidious. They don't like to use dirty, stinky litter boxes, yet they can't flush their toilet like you do. Get into the habit of being a clean-litter machine and scooping your cat's litter box every day.

You may need to try different types of boxes to find your cat's preference. Some cats like the covered models; others would rather use a wide, shallow one. If you have more than one cat, provide one litter box for each cat, plus an extra one. That may seem like a lot, but cats are territorial, and giving them choices may prevent them from using a spot behind the sofa or in your closet as a bathroom. Place litter boxes in a spot that offers some privacy.

Fill each box with two to three inches of litter. There are many litter choices, and again, some cats have strong preferences. Avoid scented litters and ones that create a lot of dust. These types are big turn-offs to most cats, who may then look elsewhere to potty.

DAILY: Scoop the urine clumps and feces into a bag you can seal and toss in the trash. Unless you're using litter specifically designed to be flushed, don't dispose of litter in the toilet, or you risk a big bill from the plumber. That will not make your parents happy.

MONTHLY: Dump the entire contents from your cat's litter box into a trash bag. Rinse out the box with hot, soapy water; dishwashing liquid is fine. Never use bleach or citrus-scented cleaners. Cats hate those strong smells. Let the litter box dry completely, then add fresh litter.

AS NEEDED: After being used for a while, a litter box becomes all scratched up, and those scratches harbor odors and germs. It's impossible to completely clean those scuffed-up boxes, so it's best to replace them.

Once your cat knows where the litter box is, you can usually count on him to use it regularly.

PET PROOF WITH A PURPOSE

You've probably heard the expression "Curiosity killed the cat." Cats love to explore their surroundings and discover new places to nap and climb. Your feline friend needs you to keep her out of trouble. In the blink of an eye, she could snag a claw in the carpet, choke on a piece of thread or dental floss, or slip out an open door.

Get in the habit of knowing where your cat is. When you leave a room and close the door behind you or close an open cupboard door, check to be sure you aren't trapping your cat in there.

KITCHEN

* Keep drawers and cupboards closed.
* A cat underfoot can trip the cook, so shoo her out when hot pans and boiling water are around.
* Keep easy-to-swallow items like twist ties and rubber bands in drawers.
* Don't leave food out. Some people foods can make cats very sick (see page 74).

OTHER ROOMS

* Check the screens in every window to make sure they are sturdy and properly installed, especially those with wide windowsills where your cat likes to roost.
* Put away potential choking hazards: game and puzzle pieces, craft projects, dangling cords.
* Keep valuable and breakable treasures in a cabinet or on a high shelf where an exploring kitty can't knock them over.
* Before sitting in a recliner or rocking chair, check to make sure your cat isn't napping underneath.

CASEY'S COMMENT

Foiled Again!

I confess. I am a feline foodie. I love, love, love to eat — even food that isn't good for me. I can leap on the kitchen counter without making a sound. But after dinner is served up, Arden puts the remaining food in the microwave to cool. She puts dirty dishes and utensils in the sink and covers it with a heavy cutting board until clean-up time. Darn it! I really want to lick those plates and sample her dinner! It smells *so* delicious!

BATHROOM AND LAUNDRY ROOM

* Keep toilet lids closed so your cat can't drink or play in the water.
* Check before closing the door when you leave.
* Store laundry supplies and cleaning materials out of reach.
* Always close the doors to the washer and dryer and check inside before using them.

What joker left the toilet lid up?

HAPPY HOLIDAYS, NOT YOWLIDAYS

Holiday celebrations, family gatherings, and other special occasions can bring lots of people (and even visiting pets) to your house. Changes in the normal household routine and decor can stoke your cat's curiosity or spike his stress level.

Here are some tips for preventing special occasions from turning into an emergency trip to the veterinary hospital.

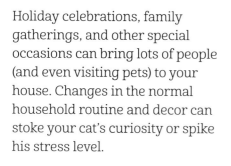

Unfair temptation!

FOR HOLIDAYS INVOLVING DECORATIONS, go with battery-operated candles to avoid flames or hot wax from harming your curious cat. Hang breakable ornaments out of reach. Don't use tinsel — it's too tempting and can cause choking if nibbled on.

Toy Patrol

Just like kids, cats often have favorite toys that they play with a lot. And some cats are really tough on toys, especially stuffed ones. When those toys become ragged and dirty, replace them. If your cat rips a hole in a soft toy, discard it and clean up any bits of stuffing that your cat might snack on.

Inspect wand toys and anything with feathers or strings. Pull off loose pieces and pick up any bits that fall to the floor during playtime. If your cat turns a feathery or fluffy toy into shreds, make a new one (see pages 109–111).

Hard plastic toys might be harboring bacteria after being batted around for a while. Replace any that are chipped or cracked.

Unfair cuteness!

GIVE YOUR CAT A SAFE PLACE to hang out when you have guests. Some social cats may want to join the fun, but a shy cat will prefer to retreat. Find a comfortable room for him, and provide him with some toys, treats, water, and a litter box. Post a "Do Not Enter — Cool Cat Inside" sign on the door to warn guests away.

KEEP FANCY FOODS OUT OF PAW'S REACH. If you have a cat who attempts to steal food on kitchen counters, confine him to a closed bedroom or other safe area away from the kitchen. See People Food: Okay or Off-Limits? (page 74) for a list of people food that isn't good for cats.

69

THE LOWDOWN ON CHOW TIME

The key to your cat's health can be found inside her food bowl. Cats are obligate carnivores, a fancy way of saying they need to eat high-quality protein to keep their muscles, organs, and bones strong. For starters, make sure your cat's food is headlined by a real meat, not by-products. The first ingredient on the label should be chicken or beef, for example, not chicken meal or meat by-products.

Don't be put off by how stinky most cat food is. Because cats don't have many taste buds compared to other mammals, their sense of smell is important in helping them pick foods to eat. Just like you, your cat has food preferences. Have you noticed how rough your cat's tongue is when she licks you? Those barbs on her tongue help her detect shapes and textures of food.

Here are a few ideas for maximizing mealtime.

SERVE MINI-MEALS. Eating two or three small meals a day helps your cat better utilize every bite of food and lessens the chances that she'll gobble too much at once and then throw it all up a few minutes later.

MEASURE, DON'T GUESS. Your veterinarian can help you figure out the correct daily portions your cat needs based on her age, health condition, and activity level.

LIMIT TREATS. If you love to give treats or are using them to train your cat, reduce her meal portions somewhat so she isn't getting too many calories. Treats should make up no more than 10 percent of your cat's daily food intake.

BE CREATIVE WITH WATER. Unlike dogs, cats are not big water gulpers, which puts them at risk for becoming dehydrated. To increase your cat's water intake, consider dishing up canned food or add a few tablespoons of sodium-free chicken or beef broth to her dry food to make it more enticing. You might consider giving your cat a water fountain that features moving water. Cats really love to paw at and drink running water.

KEEP IT CLEAN. Clean cat bowls after each meal so they don't become coated with salmonella, a nasty bacterium that can make your cat sick to her stomach. Rinse out and refill the water bowl every day, too.

Many cats love to paw at and drink running water.

THE WET vs. DRY DEBATE

People have different opinions when it comes to feeding their cats wet food or dry food or a combination of both. Some cats like the crunch of dry food, and others like the soft texture of canned food. Most veterinary nutritionists agree that you can let your cat decide, as long as you are offering a high-quality food where the main ingredient is protein, not carbohydrates. There are many special types of feline diets available. Talk to your veterinarian about the best choice for your cat.

DRY FOOD

PROS	CONS
Usually costs less than equal-quality wet food	May contain fillers or carbohydrates that provide bulk but not much nutrition
Doesn't need to be refrigerated and won't spoil or dry out if left in bowl	Contains far less moisture, so cats need to drink more water to stay properly hydrated
A large quantity can be left out if you have to be away all day or overnight	More likely to cause weight gain, especially if bowl is always full

WET FOOD

PROS	CONS
Contains more moisture, so cats are likely to stay hydrated	May cost more than equal-quality dry food
Stronger aroma and tastier texture may attract older or fussier eaters	Unserved portions must be refrigerated; uneaten portions may need to be thrown out
Makes it easier to give some medications	Smellier and messier

ASK THE VET

Why do some cats pant?

— Sadie, age 7, Chicago, Illinois

Have you ever seen a sweaty cat? I bet not! That's because cats don't sweat like people do. While cats may sweat a little bit from their paws, it's not enough to cool them off when the weather gets hot. Cats cool themselves down when it gets hot outside by panting. By breathing in cool air and panting to release the warm air, they circulate air through their bodies. It's like feline air-conditioning.

— Dr. Lisa Lippman, house call veterinarian, New York, New York

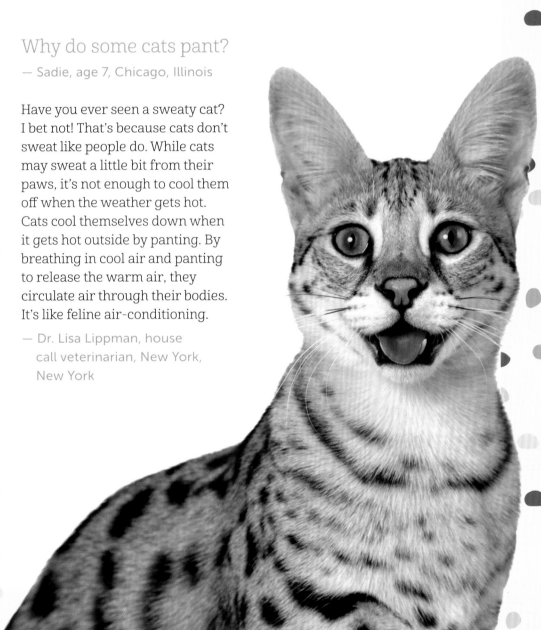

PEOPLE FOOD: OKAY OR OFF-LIMITS?

Some cats have an appetite for people food. You would expect them to beg for a piece of your turkey sandwich or crave a slice of ham, but some feline food fads are surprising. Even though they lack the taste buds for sweetness, some cats will go after fruit or ice cream. Once in a while, it is okay to offer your cat a little bit of what you are eating, but the key is *once in a while* and *a little bit*. Make sure to only offer a safe treat — some foods that are good for you aren't healthy for your cat. Here are 10 safe choices and 10 unsafe ones.

CASEY'S COMMENT

A Wide, Flat Bowl for Me!

We cats sport long whiskers. We use them to navigate, but at mealtime, our whiskers can get scrunched if we try to eat out of deep bowls. That is not a pleasant experience, trust me. I am glad that Arden serves my meals in a wide, flat bowl made out of stainless steel. It's durable and easy for her to clean, but more important, I can easily enjoy every morsel without irritating my magnificent whiskers.

OKAY

* Cooked chicken or fish
* Cooked beef (no fat or gristle)
* Sour cream
* Yogurt
* Scrambled egg
* Apple slice
* Melon
* Banana
* Asparagus (cooked)
* Cheese (small cube)

OFF-LIMITS

* Uncooked egg
* Ham and other fatty meats
* Sushi
* Avocado
* Macadamia nuts
* Chocolate
* Onion
* Raisins
* Grapes
* Coffee

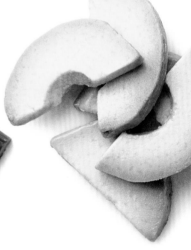

Grow Some Cat Grass

Shallow dish or flower pot

Potting soil

Packet of cat grass seed (available at many garden centers)

Cats love to nibble on grass to aid their digestion. Provide a little indoor garden by planting a pot of cat grass. You can start a new one every couple of weeks to keep a steady supply going.

THE REAL SCOOP ON MILK AND TUNA

It may surprise you that most cats lack the enzymes needed to properly digest the lactose found in milk. After lapping up a bowl of milk, your cat could develop diarrhea and stomach cramps. Nondairy milks are a no-no, too; most are loaded with sugar that is bad for a cat's teeth. A healthier alternative to offer your cat on special occasions is a dab of yogurt. Yogurt is easier than milk to digest and has healthy bacteria that are good for digestion.

So, resist those begging eyes of your cat when you are finishing a bowl of cereal. Don't put down your bowl for her to lap up the remaining milk — for her health's sake!

In general, tuna is considered safe to give your cat in moderation. There's no health harm in adding a teaspoon of canned tuna to your cat's food. But not all tuna is good for cats. Make sure you offer 100 percent tuna with no seasonings. The healthiest choice is tuna packed in water, not oil, which can be too greasy for some cats' tummies.

A fishy favorite is bonito tuna flakes, available at pet supply stores and online pet retailers. They are light as a feather, have a beckoning smell cats adore, and won't pack on the pounds.

Never feed a cat milk.

Tuna is okay in small amounts.

PICA SPELLS PERIL

Some cats intentionally chew on and sometimes ingest nonfood items. This odd eating habit, called *pica*, can lead to life-threatening internal blockages that require surgery to remove. Why do some cats nibble on sweaters, lick plastic bags, or chew on shoelaces or rubber bands? Possible reasons for pica include:

YOUTHFUL CURIOSITY. Pica in kittens may be due to exploratory behavior. Pica can begin as play with the kitten investigating and chewing on nonfood objects. Eventually, he may start eating them.

MAKING UP FOR A NUTRITIONAL LACK. Consult your veterinarian about switching to a high-fiber cat food.

SOMETHING IN THE GENE POOL. Oriental breeds, such as Siamese and Burmese, are more prone to sucking and chewing on wool than other breeds.

ENTICING AROMA. Some cats like to lick plastic bags. The surprising reason? With that powerful sense of smell, they can smell the animal product used to make the bags.

If you suspect that your cat has consumed a nonfood item, alert your parents immediately so they can check with your veterinarian. Help your cat break this dangerous habit by keeping tempting objects such as string, yarn, and dental floss out of paw's reach. Make sure your houseplants are safe for nibbling (see page 55) and offer a safe alternative, such as cat grass grown indoors (see page 75) or catnip (see page 78).

CRAZY FOR CATNIP

One out of two cats goes bonkers for this fragrant herb. The active ingredient — an oil called nepetalactone — causes them to roll on the ground, leap in the air, sprint back and forth, yowl, and/or rub their chins all over everything when they get a whiff of catnip sprinkled on their scratching post or stuffed inside a toy mouse.

Don't worry. Catnip is not harmful to your cat, and the effect lasts between 3 and 15 minutes. Organic catnip is usually more potent. A member of the mint family, catnip is easy to grow. Here are a few things to know.

✳ Catnip is a perennial that can take over a lot of space, so plant it in a large pot or somewhere where you don't mind it spreading.

✳ This herb fares best in good soil with full sun exposure.

✳ It blooms in mid- to late summer. The flowers, leaves, and stems are all safe for cats. Offer some freshly picked and dry some for a winter treat.

TO HANG DRY. Cut several bunches of stems, leaves, and flowers. Tie them in bundles with yarn and hang them in a cool, dark place with the flowers pointing down. When the leaves are dry enough to crumble between your fingers, crush the plants into a plastic bag or glass jar. Keep in a cool, dry place for up to 6 months.

TO OVEN DRY. Spread the catnip bunches out on baking sheets. Bake at the lowest setting for a few hours until dry and crumbling. Store as above.

DIY

Sock-It-to-Me Catnip Toy

Toilet paper tube

Sock

½ cup dried organic catnip

Slide the toilet paper tube inside the
sock. Add the catnip. Securely tie
the loose end of the sock into a knot.

 DiY
Cardboard Ring Toss

Paper towel tube

Scissors

Cut the tube into sections 1 to 2 inches long. Fringe the ends of the sections and fold them out as shown. Decorate as desired.

Cardboard Ring Ball

Toilet paper tube

Scissors

Small cat treats

Cut the roll into four equal-sized rings. Insert the first ring into the second and then add the third and fourth to create a hollow ball. Drop a few treats into the ball and roll it toward your cat.

Treat Puzzle Toy

Toilet paper tube

Scissors

Small cat treats

Cut two or three holes along the length of the tube, making them just a little bit bigger than the treats.

This will allow treats to fall out when your cat paws at the tube or tosses it in the air. Decorate the tube with a funny cat face or however you want.

Fold down the sides of one end of the tube to close it. Drop a few cat treats into the tube and fold the other end shut.

ASK THE VET

I love giving my sweet cat, Pumpkin, lots of treats. How many treats are too many for her? I don't want her to have a tummy ache.

— Kelly, age 10, Crown Point, Indiana

Pumpkin is lucky to be so loved by a great kid like you. You are smart to worry that too many treats can give her a tummy ache and make her overweight. If you want to give Pumpkin lots of treats, try this: Measure out Pumpkin's dry food for the day. Give her half of it in the bowl, like you normally do, and save the other half to give her as special treats. That way, you have lots of treats to give Pumpkin and she will not get sick. And stick these treats in a food puzzle so she has to use her terrific feline hunting skills to access them. But the very best treat that you can give Pumpkin is spending time with her and showing her lots of love.

— Dr. Liz Bales, Red Lion Veterinary Hospital, New Castle, Delaware

OH, BEHAVE, KITTY!

You may view certain feline actions as bad behavior, but your cat probably regards the same actions as totally acceptable. Even though cats are more independent than dogs, they are smart enough to understand and follow the rules. Harmony in the household is important for everyone, and if your cat is doing something you (or your parents) disapprove of, you can retrain him.

Here's a rundown of four common feline behaviors that often drive cat owners crazy and how you can deal with them.

EARLY ALARM

A half hour before your alarm goes off, your wide-awake cat paws your cheek, purrs loudly in your ear, walks across your stomach, bats at the window blinds, or starts knocking objects off your nightstand.

WHY? He has learned that when you're awake, you feed him. He figures, Why not eat an earlier breakfast?

Maybe the hundredth try is the charm.

CASEY'S COMMENT

Keep Your Eyes Shut!

I hate to rat out my feline friends, but here's an important tip about stopping unwanted behavior: Ignore all those attention-getting actions. If you pet your cat or get up to feed him when he wakes you up, you are rewarding him for pestering you! Put your head under the covers and pretend you're asleep. At first the behavior will get worse, but if you persist, your cat will eventually learn that he won't get an immediate response and needs to learn patience.

THE FIX: First, if you're in the habit of feeding your cat as soon as you wake up, stop! Instead, do a few morning chores, like dressing and packing up for school, before heading to the kitchen.

The next step is to reset your cat's inner clock so you can sleep later. If you feed him later at night, he won't be as hungry early in the morning. Slowly move his dinner hour closer to your bedtime by feeding him 10 or 15 minutes later than the normal time for few days. Then add another 10 or 15 minutes for a few more days, and so on, until he's adjusted to the new routine.

COUNTERTOP CRUISER

Your cat is like a magician. One second, he is sweetly rubbing against your legs, and the next, he is on the kitchen counter or surveying the scene from on top of the refrigerator.

WHY? Cats love to view the world from the safety of high places. And the kitchen is full of enticing odors, especially when someone is making turkey or ham sandwiches. He figures he might as well check out those counters just in case something tasty was left out. You can shoo your cat off whenever you see him up there, but plenty of cats figure out that they can cruise the counters when no one is looking.

THE FIX: Make those high places in your kitchen less welcoming to your cat with one of these methods:

* Place rimmed baking sheets on the counter and pour a little water into them. The next time your cat leaps onto the counter, he is surprised with a splash.

* Purchase a motion-detection canister that emits a burst of compressed air when activated. Cats hate the noise and that gust of air. Or buy a low-voltage electric mat that makes feline paws tingle unpleasantly.

* To keep him off the fridge, put out a layer of double-sided tape. The sticky texture is irritating to your cat's paws.

At the same time that you are employing these feline booby traps, redirect your cat to more acceptable places to roost. Offer him a sturdy, tall cat tree in the corner of the family room or install a wide shelf on a windowsill where he can survey the world. Look for a perching spot on top of a bookshelf or cabinet where he can't knock anything over.

AMBUSHING ANKLES

As you walk down the hallway to go to your room, your excited cat suddenly leaps out of nowhere and wraps his paws around your ankles, then gleefully sprints away.

WHY? This behavior is the ultimate game of waiting, stalking, and pouncing on prey. It occurs more with kittens who are just learning how to hunt and will react to anything — or anyone — that moves. In his mind, it's all in fun, but sharp teeth and claws are no fun for you!

THE FIX: Try to prevent the problem by engaging your cat's prey drive and use up excess energy by playing with him regularly. Drag some string for him to chase or make some toys to entertain him (see pages 79–82 and 109–111). This classic redirection technique encourages your cat to pursue more appropriate prey than your ankle.

You can also outfox your feline by offering an alternative. Make a habit of carrying a small cat toy, a wad of paper, or a ball of aluminum foil. Keep an eye out for that stalking kitty; before he can pounce, toss the toy for him to chase instead.

THE SOFA SCRATCHER

The sides and arms of padded furniture are irresistible to many cats, who dig in with gusto, usually to the horror of the family (or the parents, at least).

WHY? Cats claim their territory by using scent glands in their claws to declare that the sofa is their property. Cats also need a scratching outlet to sharpen their claws. This behavior is natural. Cats can't be trained not to scratch.

THE FIX: Offer plenty of acceptable scratching alternatives. Place a sturdy scratching post or tree near the favored pieces of furniture. There are many different models; try a few to see which entices your cat. (See page 90 for one DIY option.) Entice your cat to the tree by sprinkling organic catnip on it. Reward him with treats and praise when he claws it.

While he gets used to the new scratching posts, make the sofa less inviting by temporarily applying double-sided tape to the sides and spraying the fabric with citronella or another scent that cats hate. (Check first to make sure this spray won't damage or discolor the fabric.)

TRIVIA QUIZ 2

1. Cats use their whiskers to do which of the following things?

A. Measure if they can fit through small openings.

B. Detect prey like mice in the dark.

C. Signal moods (content, alert, threatened).

D. All of the above.

E. None of the above.

2. In ancient Egypt, cats were treated royally. What did people do to show their sadness when a beloved cat died?

A. Planted catnip.

B. Ate only sardines for a week.

C. Shaved their eyebrows.

E. Wore a sad-face mask.

3. When a cat whips his tail back and forth, what is he is saying?

A. I'm happy.

B. I'm bored.

C. I'm feeling cross.

D. I'm curious.

See page 138 for the answers.

DiY
Scratching Posts

These simple versions are just two of the hundreds of ways to build a cat scratching post. The important thing is to make sure it won't tip over. A little catnip sprinkled on the scratching surface should be all you need to interest your cat in sharpening her claws.

Add some dangly toys for added interest.

Concrete tube form (available at hardware stores)

Small area rug

Double-sided carpet tape or heavy-duty glue

Catnip

Line up the rug with the bottom of the tube. Wrap the rug around the tube, overlapping if needed.

Fasten the rug to the tube (use lots of tape or glue!).

Fold any extra rug into the top of the tube and fasten in place.

Large, sturdy cardboard box

Small area rug

Double-sided carpet tape or heavy-duty glue

Catnip

Cut the box along one side and glue or tape down the flaps. Fold the box into a triangle by overlapping two of the sides. Fasten into place.

Tape or glue the rug onto the box, tucking in the edges if needed.

Add a blanket and toys to make a cozy hidey-hole!

3

SCHOOL TIME
for Your Cat

You and your cat share a lot in common. For example, you both love to learn and discover new things. You just attend different types of schools. Your cat's classroom is inside your home, and you are his supportive teacher!

Cats are observational learners. They pay close attention to sights, sounds, smells, and household routines. That explains why they come racing into the kitchen when they hear a can being opened but stay nestled on the sofa when your cell phone rings.

HERE ARE THREE REASONS TO TRAIN YOUR CAT.

1 Get his body moving and his brain revving.

2 Build a stronger friendship and trust with him.

3 Boost his self-confidence (or give a confident cat a chance to show off).

SET UP FOR SUCCESS

Cats are just as smart as dogs, but they respond differently to training. For one thing, they are less motivated by pleasing you and more interested in earning delicious treats. To set you and your cat up for learning success, practice what I call the Three Cs of training cats: be clear, concise, and consistent. Even though your cat can't speak English, she is very good at reading your body posture and the tone of your voice and guessing what you're trying to tell her.

BE CLEAR. When training a behavior, break it into small steps so that your cat understands what you're asking for. Only give a reward when you get the behavior you want. If you say *Sit* and then reward your cat for looking at you, she's going to think that *Sit* means "Look at me."

BE CONCISE. Don't keep repeating a cue over and over. Give your cat time to think and figure out what you want.

BE CONSISTENT. Training a behavior takes a lot of repetition. Aid your cat by using the same spoken cues and gestures each and every time. Keep a cue to one or two words — *Sit* is easier to understand than *Take a seat*.

Here are a few more tips for training your cat.

PICK THE RIGHT TIME. Don't wake your cat up from a nap expecting her to happily join in a training session. Engage her attention when she's awake and ready for fun. She'll pay a lot more attention if you time your training sessions before mealtime, not right after she's eaten.

DON'T OVERDO IT. Keep training sessions short. Aim for 5 to 10 minutes once or twice a day.

DO USE TREATS. Entice your cat to learn by offering top-quality treats, such as boiled chicken or turkey cut into itty-bitty pieces.

LOCATION IS KEY. Pick a quiet place free of distractions so you both can focus.

MAKE LEARNING FUN. Be encouraging and full of happy praise. Stop the lesson if you start to get frustrated or impatient or if your cat gets bored or confused. She will tell you by abruptly leaving the room or beginning to groom herself.

Strive to end on a good note. If your cat aces a cue three times in a row, it's time to stop, give one more treat, and celebrate.

CASEY'S COMMENT

Need a Translator?

I'm here to tell you that cats are bilingual. We speak cat, of course, and we also must learn a little of whatever language our human family speaks. As for me, I am a trilingual feline. I speak cat, English, and sign language. In our pet first-aid and pet behavior classes, Arden asks me to sit and come and touch paws by speaking the words and, sometimes, by only using hand signals. I love hearing the applause from the students . . . and getting those yummy treats, of course!

ASK THE VET

Do cats always land on their feet from a high fall?

— Cailyn, age 10, Davenport, Iowa

Much like Olympic gymnasts, cats exhibit a keen sense of orientation when twisting in midair. The cats' flexible spine, strong muscles, and great balance enable them most of the time to land safely with all four feet touching the ground.

Cats do not have collarbones, so their backbones are more mobile and flexible than those of people or dogs, enabling them to rotate their bodies easily. When a cat senses that he is falling, his brain communicates to the muscles to alert them to twist in such a way that the cat's head is parallel to the ground. When this is accomplished, the cat's body naturally follows to enable the cat to land upright.

But as agile as cats are, they do not always escape injury from falls out open windows, off balconies, and from rooftops. Take precautions to keep your curious cat safe.

— Dr. Nicholas Dodman, veterinarian and professor emeritus, Cummings School of Veterinary Medicine at Tufts University, North Grafton, Massachusetts

SCHOOL IS IN SESSION!

On the next pages you'll find step-by-step guides to teach your cat to come, shake paws, circle, and jump through a hoop. You'll have fun impressing your family and friends with your circus cat act!

TEACHING COME

For your cat's safety, teach him to come when he hears his name called. Your curious cat may have found a new hiding spot in the house — like behind the refrigerator or in a closet — or somehow have slipped outside. If he will respond to your call, you have a better chance of finding him. And you can call him to come when you want to teach him other tricks.

1 **Begin training just before mealtimes, when your cat is ready to pay attention.** Cats quickly recognize the sound of a can opener or a flip-top lid being popped, so as you open a can of food, call his name (you can also rattle some kibble or a bag of cat treats): "Here, Mikey, Mikey, Mikey!"

Or use a signal, like a whistle or tapping a spoon on a can, that you want him to associate with food.

2 **When your cat comes running for his meal, give him a special treat.** Then put down his bowl. Practice this at every meal for a while, until he knows that your voice calling or whistling always means there's a yummy treat in store.

3 **Now start calling him in between mealtimes.** Reward him whether he comes running or just strolling.

You can't expect a cat to dash over every time you call, but if you make it worth his while, you might be surprised at the response!

TEACHING SIT

Teaching your cat to sit is the basis for many other tricks. Once he's mastered it, try holding the treat higher over his head while saying *Beg* or *Paws up* and waiting for him to reach for it.

1 **Get your cat's attention** by showing him that you have some delicious treats.

Hold a treat in front of his face, then slowly lift it over his head as you say *Sit*.

2 **Ideally, as he follows the treat with his nose,** his head will go up and his butt will sit.

Immediately reward him by saying *Good sit* and handing over the treat.

3 **Your cat may bat at your hand to get at the treat** or even sit up on his hind legs. Be patient until he puts his front paws down, then reward him.

Keep practicing until he makes the connection between your saying *Sit* and your hand gesture over his head.

TEACHING SHAKE

Cats often investigate the world by pawing at things they are curious about. This is a fun trick to teach a social cat who already knows how to sit.

1 **Have your cat at eye level,** either with you sitting on the floor or with him on a table facing you. Ask him to *Sit*.

CASEY'S COMMENT

I'm a Lefty!

Just like people, cats are right- or left-handed, or rather, -pawed. Although we are quite talented in using all our paws, we usually have one we favor more to reach for treats, step into the litter box with, or raise to say hi. As for me, I'm a lefty, which makes me a southpaw!

2 Hold a treat a couple of inches in front of his eyes and say *Shake*. When he lifts a front paw to grab the treat, say *Good shake* and give him the treat.

Repeat this over several sessions until he lifts his paw whenever your hand is at his eye level.

3 Now begin to gently touch his raised paw with the hand that holds the treat to complete the handshake. Hand over the treat when you've touched his paw.

TEACHING CIRCLE

If your cat loves to follow you and is eager to learn new things, you can probably teach him to walk in a complete circle on cue. You'll need a target stick, which is just a long dowel or the handle of a wooden spoon with one end covered in something your cat likes, such as a dab of butter or smear of soft cheese.

1 Start with your cat sitting facing you. Position the stick, loaded with a treat, at your cat's nose and let him lick off the treat.

Repeat this a few times (reloading the stick each time) so that he learns to pay attention to the stick.

2 Keeping the loaded target stick at your cat's head level, slowly move it away from him. As soon as he takes a few steps to follow the treat, stop, let him have the treat, and praise.

3 Gradually make your cat take more steps before treating and praising, until he will follow the stick in a full circle.

4 Now you are ready to mark the action with a verbal cue. Say *Circle* as you move the target stick in a circle.

As soon as your cat completes the rotation, treat and say *Good circle*. Once your cat is consistently circling, you can replace the target stick with your hand holding a treat.

TEACHING
JUMP THROUGH A HOOP

If you have an outgoing feline performer, you can me-WOW your friends by having your cat leap through a hula hoop as you hold it off the ground. Make sure your cat knows how to follow a target stick (or your hand holding a treat) before trying this more advanced trick. You'll need a hula hoop or something similar.

1 **Face your cat with the hoop between you.** At first, rest the hoop on the floor. Load a stick with a treat (see page 104).

2 Coax your cat to follow the target stick through the hoop to get the treat. Start with the hoop resting on the ground.

Praise and say *Hoop* each time he walks through, so he starts to associate the word *hoop* with the desired action.

3 Once he is comfortable walking through, start to raise the hoop slightly off the ground. Start at just an inch or two, then slowly increase the height as he learns what to do.

You will probably need several training sessions to build up your cat's confidence and willingness.

CASEY RIDES IN STYLE

Because Arden takes me to pet conferences and classrooms to teach people all about cats, I leaped on her offer to teach me to ride in a pet stroller. She started by parking the stroller with the lid up in the middle of the living room. That caught my curiosity, and of course I had to explore it. When she tossed a couple of treats inside, I eagerly jumped in it to gobble them up. The next day she started to feed me my breakfast in the stroller.

After I proved I liked the stroller, she gently pushed it around the house with me inside, occasionally stopping to hand me a treat. She gave me time to trust the stroller and welcome the motion.

We both like the stroller for different reasons. Instead of being jolted inside a moving pet carrier, I enjoy a smooth and dignified ride. For Arden, pushing the stroller is a breeze compared to having to muscle the heavy pet carrier. It's a win-win!

A couple more tips to set you and your cat up for success: For safety reasons, make sure your cat is wearing a harness with the built-in stroller leash fastened to the D ring on the harness. And keep the mesh lid on the stroller down so your cat can still see his surroundings but can't try to leap out. Ride on!

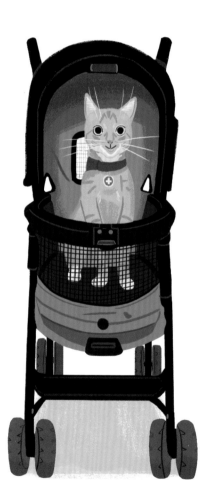

Wave-a-Wand Toy

Cats love to chase, pounce, and leap after moving things. Here and on the next two pages are some simple toys to entice them to play.

Sturdy stick or dowel, 24–36 inches long

Thick yarn or string

Small cat toy, yarn pom-pom, or crumpled wad of paper

1 Tie one end of the string to the stick and tie the toy, pom-pom, or paper wad onto the other end of the string. Have fun experimenting with different toys and lengths of string.

2 Drag the toy across the floor or flick it in the air for your cat to leap after.

Fleece Ring Toy

Scraps of fleece, felt, or other thick fabric in various colors

Scissors or rotary cutter

1 Cut one strip of fabric about 6 inches long and 1 inch wide. Tie the ends together to form a circle.

2 Cut 12 to 15 strips of fabric about 3 inches long and ½ inch wide. Tie these strips onto the circle, using double knots to secure them.

3 Wiggle the toy or toss it across the floor for your cat. Or tie it on a long string and drag it like a moving mouse.

DiY
Dangling Doorknob Toy

Small toy mouse or crumpled wad of paper

Strip of thick fabric 12–15 inches long and about 1 inch wide

1 Securely tie the toy or paper wad to one end of the fabric strip.

2 Tie the other end of the fabric strip around an interior room doorknob so that it dangles 6 to 8 inches off the ground — about eye level to your cat.

3 Move the toy back and forth to attract your cat. You may have to drag it on the floor. Be sure he watches you fasten it to the doorknob.

BE YOUR CAT'S

Best Health Ally

You play many key roles for your feline friend. You are his cuddle buddy, play pal, chief caretaker, and all-important pooper-scooper. All of these roles help you bring out the best in your cat and keep tabs on his health and surroundings. Another important role is pet health detective, where you keep an eye out for clues on your cat's well-being.

In addition to covering some first-aid and general health-care tips, this chapter spotlights the benefits of playtime. To stay healthy and happy, cats need to have their brains and bodies exercised regularly. Let the good times roll!

FUN AND GAMES

As we've discussed, a bored cat is apt to get into feline mischief. And an overweight cat is at risk for a host of health conditions, like arthritis and diabetes. That's why it's important for you to play with your cat to get her moving. Try these games to see which ones your cat enjoys the most. Then make up some new ones!

FOOD SCAVENGER HUNT

Appeal to your cat's inner hunter by introducing her to a food scavenger hunt at least once a week. Skip the food bowl for one meal, instead hiding kibble or small bowls of wet food in several different places or on a few steps going up the staircase.

After you hide the food, call your cat to you. You may have to guide her to the first food find, but then stand back and watch her sense of smell and hunting instincts take over. Be sure to remove all of the hidden food once your cat has finished eating.

MURPHY IN THE MIDDLE

I named this game in honor of my late great black feline, who loved to leap and grab at flying objects in midair. You need another person to play with and a few small toys or wads of paper, something you know your cat will chase.

Start with you and your friend sitting about 10 feet apart with the cat in the middle. Spark your cat's interest by crinkling the paper wad or dangling the toy. Then toss it to your friend about a foot above the cat's head for her to grab at. You'll know when the game is over when your cat walks away or turns her back and starts to groom herself.

FISH IN THE BAG

Cats can't resist exploring empty paper grocery bags left on the kitchen floor. Make it even more fun by setting up some indoor "fishing"!

If the bag has handles, play it safe by cutting them off so your cat won't get caught in them. Next, cut a circle in the bottom of the bag. Tie a small toy or paper wad to one end of a shoelace or piece of heavy string to serve as your fishing line and bait. Insert the toy through the hole until it is about halfway inside the bag. Lay the bag on its side with the bottom facing you.

Place your cat at the open end and wiggle the bait to encourage her to dive into the bag to capture her prey. As she dives into the bag, reel the bait out of the hole. Timing is important — see if you can be quicker than she is!

TUB HOCKEY

If your cat loves to chase balls and toys, you can create a hockey rink to show off her athletic skills. Just toss a small object in an empty bathtub. Feline favorites are table tennis balls, crinkly foil pom-poms, and plastic rings from milk jugs.

Toss the object so it makes noise as it rolls around the interior sides of the bathtub. Praise your cat each time she gives pursuit.

IT'S A (TOWEL) WRAP!

Cats can be more difficult than dogs to restrain for several reasons. In general, cats receive less socialization and handling than dogs. In addition, their evolutionary history as a prey species can cause them to feel more vulnerable when held in place and not allowed to flee. When it comes to giving cats medicine or trimming their nails, safety is paramount for both of you. You don't want to wind up with scratched arms or legs — ouch! A good solution is to wrap your cat in a bath towel, with the help of an adult.

Pet experts advise against "scruffing" a cat by grabbing the back of its neck in order to give medicine or trim nails. An irate or panicky cat can quickly maneuver his flexible spine so that his back claws leave you bloodied as he wiggles free and flees. Toweling is preferred by veterinarians and technicians to safely control an ill or injured cat. It's ideal for cats who tend to be anxious, fearful, or aggressive when handled.

Wrapping your cat in a large bath towel has three benefits.

* It protects you from sharp claws and teeth.

* It holds the patient still for medication.

* It helps calm a frightened feline.

Here's the key: you must introduce the towel in a positive way. Your goal is to have the cat accept being wrapped and restrained. Practice this technique when your cat is calm so that he's used to it when you need to wrap him. It's good to do this with adult help until you are comfortable and your cat is more accepting. Use lots of treats and praise and restrain your cat for just a few seconds at first. If you let him go a few times without doing anything else, he'll learn that being wrapped isn't so awful!

CAT-WRAPPING TECHNIQUE

Here is your step-by-step guide to what is popularly known as the "purrito" (or kitty burrito) toweling technique.

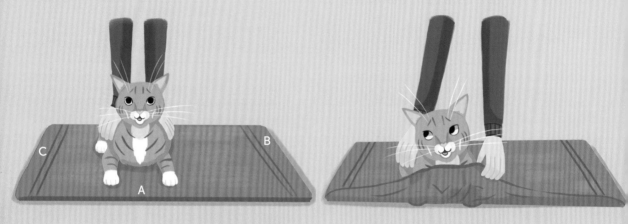

1 **Place your cat** several inches from the long side of the towel (A) and about a foot from one of the short ends (C).

2 **Tuck the edge** of the long side (A) over the paws and around the neck.

3 **Pull the longer side** of the towel (B) over your cat, covering his whole body.

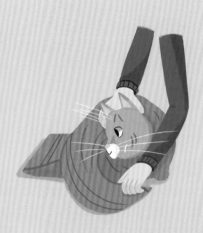

4 Then pull the corner of the towel forward and wrap it under the chin, like a scarf.

5 Once the towel is wrapped all the way around, take the shorter side (C) and pull it over the cat. Make it snug and keep it in place by holding on firmly so your cat can't wiggle out.

Success! Your cat is now safely secured in the towel and ready to receive pills or liquid medications or to have his nails trimmed (see page 120).

NAIL-TRIMMING TIME

If you have a kitten, start right away touching her paws and lightly pressing on her pads to expose her claws. Do it in a fun way, for just a few seconds at a time at first, and always dole out some delicious treats. This will make nail-trimming sessions more pleasant for the both of you. A mellow older cat might be willing to learn this, but for a feisty cat, it may be safer to have nail-trimming done by a veterinary technician during a health visit or by a professional groomer.

Home Paw-dicure

Nail trimming at home is easier if one person holds the cat while the other uses the clippers. If your feline is receptive, give it a try. Set out the grooming tools in the bathroom or other enclosed space so your cat can't escape. You will need a thick towel, nail clippers, and styptic powder in case you accidentally cut a nail too short and it bleeds. Don't forget some treats!

1 **Wrap your cat in a bath towel** (see page 118), then gently pull out one paw at a time from the towel to trim nails.

2 **Place your thumb on top of the paw** with your fingers on the pads. Gently press the pads one at a time to expose the claws.

3 **Snip just the tip of the claw —** the clear, white part. The pink area is called the quick and is where the vein that runs through the claw ends. It will bleed if cut.

Phew, I made it!

Talk calmly to your cat while trimming. When you're done, unwrap the towel and hand out a tasty treat or two. You want your cat to have a positive experience. It may take a few sessions for her to realize that nothing terrible has happened!

HOW TO PLAY PET HEALTH DETECTIVE

Go away. There's nothing to see here.

Unlike dogs, who generally let you know when they don't feel well or are injured, cats tend to hide any signs of pain or weakness. That's why it is important to be on the lookout for clues that may indicate your cat is not his usual healthy self.

Ask yourself these questions.

* Is there a change in litter box habits?

* Is his appetite off?

* Is he hiding when he is usually outgoing?

* Is he swatting or hissing when you attempt to pick him up?

* Is he scratching a lot or chewing on his paws?

These are all clues alerting you that something is wrong, so let your parents know that you're worried.

LEARN PET FIRST AID

One of the best ways to show your cat just how much you love him is to take a pet first-aid class. Kids are often welcome to join their parents at these classes. Here are three reasons why you should learn pet first aid.

* You will learn how to stay calm and focused when your cat is ill or injured.

* You will help your family save money on veterinary bills by catching your cat's health issues early.

* You will learn what to do in a particular emergency to possibly save your cat's life.

By taking a class, you will learn how to help a cat who is choking or has been stung by a bee. You will also learn how to stop the bleeding on a paw, give liquid medicine, perform rescue breathing and CPR (cardiopulmonary resuscitation), and much, much more!

123

ASK THE VET

How can cats jump so high when they are so small?

— Regan, age 8, Seattle, Washington

Cats can jump so high because they have incredibly large and well-developed thigh muscles for their size. When they crouch and push off, it's like they are being catapulted through the air!

If your legs were equally powerful, you could jump from the ground to the top of your house with ease. But your thigh muscles would be as big around as your waist!

— Dr. Marty Becker, America's Family Veterinarian, Bonners Ferry, Idaho

CHECK YOUR CAT FROM EARS TO TAIL

Practice prevention by performing a full-body wellness checkup on your cat every month. This is a wonderful way to bond with your kitty while you are on the lookout for health issues. Start by drawing three outlines of your cat's body: a side view, belly view, and head view. You will use these drawings to mark places where your cat may have a problem like a bump or lump, a cut, a rash, or evidence of fleas.

Gather a handful of your cat's favorite treats (tiny pieces of broiled chicken are a true feline favorite!). Bring your cat to a small room that is free from distractions, like the bathroom or a quiet bedroom, and that has a door you can close. Place your cat on the bathroom counter or the bed and offer her a treat. Turn the page for a checkup checklist.

Snuggles afterward, right?

KITTY WELLNESS CHECK

Write down any findings on your drawing and share them with your parents. Make this process something your cat looks forward to each time by finishing your at-home wellness exam with healthy treats and praise.

Start your checkup at your cat's head. First, lightly touch her nose. A healthy nose is dry or slightly moist. An unhealthy nose might be very dry and scaly or, worse, full of mucus.

Slowly move a treat from side to side in front of her eyes. You are checking if she moves her head and eyes to follow its direction. (Watch out for her trying to grab the treat with a front paw!)

Are her pupils the same size? If one pupil is smaller or larger than the other, it could signal a medical problem that you need to share with your parents — and your veterinarian.

Gently fold back each ear and peek inside. You want to see a nice pink color, not bright red. Give a sniff, too. Dark brown dirt that looks like coffee grounds and/or a smell like dirty socks may mean an ear infection or ear mites.

Examine each paw and paw pad for cuts, nails that have grown too long, or (yuck) ticks between the toes.

Slowly glide your hand from her head down to the base of her tail. Then gently massage her skin with your fingertips. Wincing or resistance may indicate a sore muscle or arthritis.

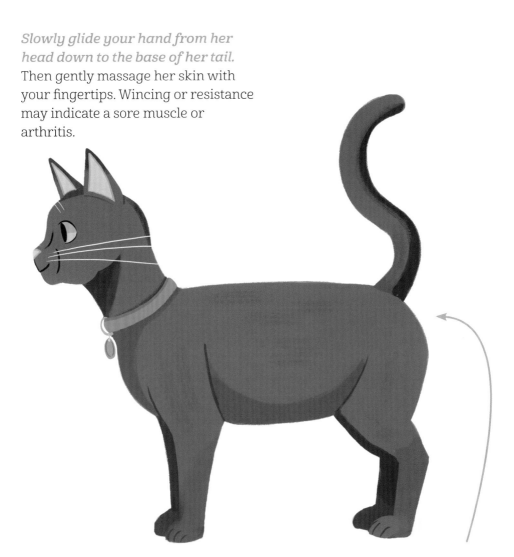

Look at her belly for any signs of redness or rashes. If she'll let you, gently feel for lumps or bumps with your open hand. Play it safe — not all cats like having their bellies touched.

Use a special flea comb to check for fleas (your veterinarian can show you how).

Gently lift her tail and check for redness or dry poop dangling, which may indicate a health problem.

Check her tail for cuts or bumps. Make sure your cat hasn't injured her tail somehow.

127

DEALING WITH PEE, POOP, PUKE, AND HAIRBALLS

You can catch some health concerns in the early stages by paying attention to and reporting any changes in your cat's "deposits."

PEE: LIQUID GOLD

Veterinarians often refer to urine as liquid gold because it can give them a lot of data about a cat's health status. Healthy feline urine should be yellow, not orange, pink, red, or brown. It should not smell strongly.

CASEY'S COMMENT

Arden Saved My Life!

We male cats sometimes suffer serious urinary blockages. One time I was having trouble peeing in my litter box. I let out a yowl because I could only urinate a little. When Arden rushed over to check the litter box, she discovered blood in my urine.

She immediately took me to the emergency veterinary clinic, where I had to stay overnight. When I was all better and Arden picked me up, the veterinarian told her that if she had waited until morning to take me, I might have died. Yikes! I'm glad she acted quickly.

Pay attention to your cat's potty habits. Be sure to report any changes in how often your cat urinates and how much. For example, if your cat usually pees three times in his litter box a day and suddenly you are finding only one urine clump or the clumps are much larger than normal, something is wrong.

BECOME A POOPOLOGIST

It's a stinky job, but an important one. You need to notice your cat's poop, or feces, each time you scoop the litter box. Healthy cat poop is chocolate brown in color and shaped like a log.

It should not:

* Resemble small hard pellets. This could indicate your kitty is suffering from constipation.

* Look like a watery, reddish brown puddle. This means your cat has diarrhea.

* Be really stinky and contain what look like coffee grounds. That could mean that your cat has internal bleeding. Take your cat to a veterinarian right away!

129

THE DIFFERENCE BETWEEN PUKE AND HAIRBALLS

Cats vomit for many reasons, including eating too quickly, eating food that is spoiled or not good for them (like milk — see page 76), or ingesting poison from a plant or medication. Some cats, like some kids, suffer from motion sickness while riding in the family vehicle.

Yes, vomit is yucky, but put your pet detective skills to use. If your cat vomits once in a great while and then goes about his normal routine, don't worry. But if he vomits more than once in a day, acts sluggish, and turns down any food offerings, play it safe and take him to the vet.

Hairballs are the number one reason why cats vomit. About 8 out of 10 cats hack up a hairball at least once a month. The usual cause is the feline beauty routine. Unlike you, your cat doesn't stay clean by showering. Instead, he meticulously grooms

The scientific name for hairball is trichobezoar.

himself by licking his fur. As he grooms, the barbs on his tongue grab loose hairs, which get swallowed. Most times, this hair passes through the digestive system without issue and exits in the poop. But a large amount of hair can gather in the cat's stomach and mix with digestive juices to form a hairball. Eventually it becomes irritating enough that the cat has to expel the fuzzy mess.

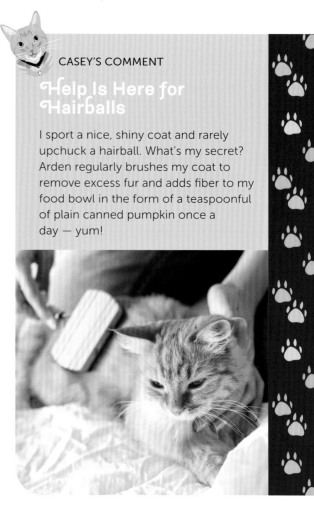

CASEY'S COMMENT

Help Is Here for Hairballs

I sport a nice, shiny coat and rarely upchuck a hairball. What's my secret? Arden regularly brushes my coat to remove excess fur and adds fiber to my food bowl in the form of a teaspoonful of plain canned pumpkin once a day — yum!

As your cat grooms herself, the barbs on her tongue grab loose hairs, which get swallowed.

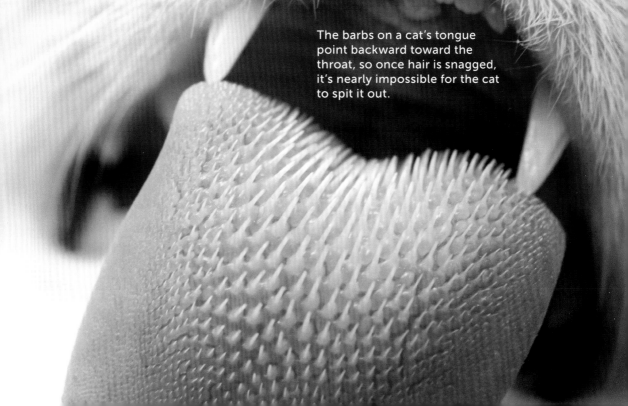

The barbs on a cat's tongue point backward toward the throat, so once hair is snagged, it's nearly impossible for the cat to spit it out.

MAKE VET VISITS LESS SCARY

Most cats prefer to be homebodies and are not big fans of car trips, especially to the veterinary clinic. To many, it represents the Three Cs of Concern: the carrier, the car ride, and the clinic. You can do your part to help make veterinary visits less scary for your cat. Here are some tips.

MAKE THE CAT CARRIER A SAFE and welcoming place for your cat by keeping it somewhere your cat likes to hang out, such as in your bedroom or a corner of the family room. Keep the carrier door open and toss a few treats inside to entice your cat to approach. Let her enter and leave as she wishes. Occasionally feed your cat inside the carrier with the door open.

ACCLIMATE YOUR CAT to traveling in the carrier by slowly getting her used to the sights and smells of the car while it's parked. Offer her a treat and bring her back in the house. After doing that a few times over several days, ask your parents to take your cat for a ride around the block to build up her exposure to traveling in the car. Going on a few short trips that end up right back at home will help her be more comfortable in the car.

KEEP YOUR CAT SAFE by placing the carrier on the floor behind the front passenger seat or by running the seat belt through the carrier's handle and snapping it in place in the back seat. Never put the carrier on the front passenger seat because in an accident, the air bags may deploy and injure your cat. Also, having a cat in the front passenger seat can be distracting for the driver.

USE CALMING SPRAYS. Pet sprays that contain pheromones, such as Feliway, help calm some cats. Be sure to spray inside the carrier as well as in your family's vehicle. These scents are not detectable by human noses.

BOOK ROUTINE APPOINTMENTS at the veterinary clinic during a slow time so you won't have to wait as long. This will prevent your cat from becoming more and more anxious or agitated if the vet is delayed.

POSITION THE CARRIER while you're waiting so your cat faces you, not other pets in the lobby. If possible, place the carrier on a level surface off the floor. Cats feel safer when they aren't on ground level.

IF YOUR CAT IS VERY NERVOUS or overly excited, ask if you can be ushered right into an exam room or stay in the car until the veterinarian is ready to see you.

USE A CALM, HAPPY VOICE to reassure your cat, but avoid baby talk. Cats read our moods very well, and you need to convey that there is no danger. In a cat's mind, a person talking in a high squeaky tone is not confident or in control of a situation. Baby talk can actually cause some cats to panic and become stressed or scared.

ASK IF YOU CAN BRING TREATS to give your cat in the exam room to distract her while being examined. Respect what the vet says. Sometimes, the best thing is for the owner to leave while a cat is having a stressful procedure, like having blood drawn or a urine sample taken. This way, you can be the good guy or gal who comforts your cat afterward.

WHEN TO TAKE
YOUR CAT TO THE VET

Beyond the obvious situations like heavy bleeding, massive trauma to the head, or a broken bone, here are some scenarios that merit a prompt trip to the veterinarian for your cat.

* Limping or unable to walk

* Difficulty breathing

* A bite from another animal, including a snake

* A deep cut or a puncture wound

* Eating poison, such as antifreeze, rat bait, or human medication (aspirin is toxic to cats)

* Unconsciousness

* Having a seizure

Choose Fear Free Handling

More veterinarians are recognizing that many cats become extremely frightened when visiting their offices. Instead of trying to scruff or restrain these "fraidy cats," many veterinarians are using safer, gentler handling techniques to greet and treat their feline patients. They are becoming certified in Fear Free handling methods designed to reduce fear, stress, and anxiety in pets as well as allow more accurate and thorough examinations.

Techniques include allowing a nervous cat to remain in the carrier as much as possible. If the carrier opens from the top, the veterinarian can do some of the exam with the cat in the carrier where it feels safer. Some cats are calmer after being swaddled in a towel. Using feline pheromone sprays in the exam room can help ease anxiety.

DiY
Pet First-Aid Kit

It is good to keep two first-aid kits in your home — one for you and your family and one for your pets. Some items in a human kit are unsafe or unnecessary to have in a pet first-aid kit. Post this number on the kit or in a handy place: ASPCA Poison Control (1-800-426-4435).

First-aid tape
(to keep bandages
in place)

Instant cold compress
(to reduce swelling)

Rubbing (isopropyl)
alcohol (to clean a
wound or sterilize a tool)

Antibiotic ointment
(to disinfect a wound)

Sting relief pads (to treat an
insect bite or sting)

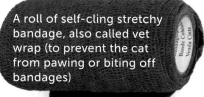

A roll of self-cling stretchy
bandage, also called vet
wrap (to prevent the cat
from pawing or biting off
bandages)

Blunt-tipped
scissors (to cut
adhesive tape
or gauze)

Gauze pads and a roll
of gauze (for cuts,
bleeding wounds, and
mild burns)

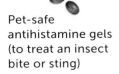

Pet-safe antihistamine gels (to treat an insect bite or sting)

Disposable, nonlatex gloves (to keep your hands clean)

Water-based lubricant (to use with the thermometer)

STYPTIC POWDER
Stops Bleeding

Styptic powder (to stop minor bleeding)

first aid
saline solution
Sterile Saline Eye Wash
ANTIBACTERIAL

Sterile saline eye wash (to flush dirt or objects from the eye)

Rectal thermometer (to measure body temperature)

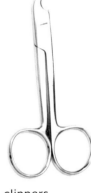

Pet nail clippers (to trim nails that are too long)

Tick removal tool (Don't use tweezers or a hot match!)

Bath towel (for wrapping — see page 118)

Restraint muzzle designed for a cat (Don't try to put this on an injured cat yourself; ask an adult.)

Answers to Trivia Quizzes

QUIZ 1 (PAGE 27)

1. **False.** Cats have a special membrane in their eyes called the tapetum lucidum that gives them better vision in the dark than humans, but they still can't navigate in the house in total darkness. They appreciate a nightlight in the hallway as much as you do!

2. **True.** Adult cats can have blue, green, brown, or yellow eyes.

3. **False.** Some cats purr when they are in a scary situation, such as at the veterinary clinic, as a way to try to calm down. Mama cats purr when they are feeding their newborn kittens.

4. **True.** One of the oldest cat breeds, the Turkish Van hails from Lake Van in Turkey. These cats learned to splash their paws in the water to hunt for fish. Modern-day Turkish Vans generally like to swim. Some even join their favorite people in the bathtub!

QUIZ 2 (PAGE 89)

1. **D.** Feline whiskers have many functions. What would it be like to have whiskers of your own?

2. **C.** Shaving the eyebrows signified a period of mourning, which ended when the hair grew back. Ancient Egyptians loved cats so much, they even worshipped a cat goddess named Bastet.

3. **C.** Furious tail-lashing is a warning sign to back away because that cat is upset or frightened and may swat or bite.

Resources

American Association of Feline
Practitioners
www.catvets.com

American Society for the Prevention
of Cruelty to Animals
www.aspca.org

American Veterinary Medical
Association
www.avma.org

Catster Magazine
www.catster.com

Cat Writers' Association, Inc
www.catwriters.com

Fear Free Happy Homes
www.fearfreehappyhomes.com

Fear Free Pets
www.fearfreepets.com

FetchFind
www.fetchfind.com

Humane Society of the United States
www.humanesociety.org

Pet First Aid 4U
www.petfirstaid4U.com

Pet Life Radio
www.petliferadio.com

Pro Pet Hero
ProTrainings
www.propethero.com

METRIC CONVERSIONS

LENGTH

TO CONVERT	TO	MULTIPLY
inches	millimeters	inches by 25.4
inches	centimeters	inches by 2.54
inches	meters	inches by 0.0254

US (INCHES)	METRIC (CENTIMETERS)
0.5	1.27
1	2.54
2	5.08
3	7.62
4	10.16
5	12.70
6	15.24

WEIGHT

TO CONVERT	TO	MULTIPLY
ounces	grams	ounces by 28.35
pounds	grams	pounds by 453.5
pounds	kilograms	pounds by 0.45

US (OUNCES)	METRIC (GRAMS)
0.035 ounce	1 gram
½ ounce	14 grams
1 ounce	28 grams
1¾ ounces	50 grams
3½ ounces	100 grams
8 ounces	228 grams
16 ounces (1 pound)	454 grams

Recommended Reading

The Original Cat Bible, Sandy Robins with Arnold Plotnick, Lorraine Shelton, and Sarah Hartwell, CompanionHouse Books, 2014

Cat Scene Investigator: Solve Your Cat's Litter Box Mystery, Dusty Rainbolt, Stupid Gravity Press, 2016

Cats for the GENIUS, Ramona D. Marek, For the GENIUS Press, 2016

Cats on the Job, Lisa Rogak, St. Martin's Griffin, 2015

How to Speak Cat, Aline Alexander Newman and Gary Weitzman, National Geographic Children's Books, 2015

OTHER CAT BOOKS BY ARDEN MOORE

The Cat Behavior Answer Book, Storey Publishing, 2007

Fit Cat: Tips and Tricks to Give Your Pet a Longer, Healthier, Happier Life, Firefly Books, 2015

Happy Cat, Happy You, Storey Publishing, 2008

Planet Cat: A CAT-alog, Arden Moore, Sandra Choron, and Harry Choron, Mariner Books, 2007

ACKNOWLEDGMENTS

I give special gratitude to all the veterinarians and cat behaviorists who have honed my knowledge of all things feline, especially Dr. Marty Becker, Dr. Elizabeth Colleran, Samantha Martin of the Amazing Acro-Cats, and Dr. Alice Moon-Fanelli.

Lastly, I give thanks to the entire Storey Publishing team, especially my main editor, Lisa Hiley, for helping me with my dream to create a cat book for kids come true.

Index

Additional photography by © 101cats/iStock.com, 26 l., 77, 139; © ablokhin/iStock.com, 17, 95; © Africa Studio/stock.adobe.com, 57; © Aksenovko/iStock.com, 130 r.; © Alena Ozerova/stock.adobe.com, 9; © AlexStepanov/iStock.com, 85; © AnatoliYakovenko/iStock.com, 93; © andy_gin/stock.adobe.com, 87; © anna1311/iStock.com, 74 (apples); © AnnaRise/iStock.com, 122; © Annashou/iStock.com, 31 l.; © Antagain/iStock.com, 1; © Arden Moore, 6; © Astrid860/iStock.com, 70; © Andrey Kuzmin/Alamy Stock Photo, 4–5; © BackyardProduction/iStock.com, 123; © baibaz/iStock.com, 74 (avocado, chocolate), 76 t.; © Benjamin Simeneta/stock.adobe.com, 68; © byallasaa/stock.adobe.com, 75; © c-foto/iStock.com, 20; © CHUYN/iStock.com, 31 c.; © cunfek/iStock.com, 60; © cynoclub/iStock.com, 32; © DebbiSmirnoff/iStock.com, 67; © DenisNata/stock.adobe.com, 33; © digihelion/iStock.com, 131 t.; © Dobroslav Hadzhiev/stock.adobe.com, 120, 121; © Ekaterina Kolomeets/stock.adobe.com, 23, 39; © Eric Isselée/stock.adobe.com, 34; © Erik Lam/stock.adobe.com, 37 l.; © Ermolaev Alexandr/stock.adobe.com, 16, 27 t., 38, 89 t., 129; © fotostok_pdv/iStock.com, 61; © GCapture/iStock.com, 15; © GlobalP/iStock.com, 11 c. & r., 71 (cat), 109 (cat); © goodwin_x/stock.adobe.com, 71 (water); © Grigorita Ko/stock.adobe.com, 47; © Happy monkey/stock.adobe.com, 125; © ingusk/stock.adobe.com, 43; © Jane Burton/Getty Images, 69; © jkitan/iStock.com, 2–3; © jptinoco/iStock.com, 117; © Juanmonino/iStock.com, 76 b.; © jumnong/stock.adobe.com, 82 (cat); © Juniors Bildarchiv GmbH/Alamy Stock Photo, 97; © KaeArt/iStock.com, 27 b.; © Katrina Brown/stock.adobe.com, 133; © Khorzhevska/stock.adobe.com, 28, 110 (cat); © Koljambus/iStock.com, 14; © Konstiantyn/stock.adobe.com, 55 b.; © kozorog/iStock.com, 26 r.; © Kurhan/stock.adobe.com, 41; © Life On White.com/Getty Images, 11 l.; © marieclaudelemay/iStock.com, 59; © Mark_KA/stock.adobe.com, 66 (cat); © Mary Swift/stock.adobe.com, 86; © Maryviolet/iStock.com, 30; © master1305/iStock.com, 124 b.; © mayakova/iStock.com, 74 (bananas); © Nils Jacobi/iStock.com, 22; © NitikornIstock/iStock.com, 84; © noreefly/stock.adobe.com, 88; © nuzza11/stock.adobe.com, 24; © Nynke van Holten/iStock.com, 73 b.; © PeopleImages/iStock.com, 42; © perets/iStock.com, 44, 45, 65; © PetrMalyshev/iStock.com, 135; © phanasitti/iStock.com, 78 l.; © pio3/stock.adobe.com, 132; © PK-Photos/iStock.com, 134; © Remains/iStock.com, 12; © RichardUpshur/iStock.com, 83 b.; © Roman Sakhno/stock.adobe.com, 94; © s_derevianko/iStock.com, 21; © schankz/stock.adobe.com, 31 r., 89 b.; © seregraff/stock.adobe.com, 13; © serkucher/stock.adobe.com, 37 r.; © silberkorn73/stock.adobe.com, 96 l.; © Sonsedska/iStock.com, 56; © Stephanie Zieber/stock.adobe.com, 81 (cat); © Syda Productions/stock.adobe.com, 46; © Tetiana Kovalenko/Alamy Stock Photo, 78 r.; © Todorean Gabriel/stock.adobe.com, 131 b.; © Tomwang112/iStock.com, 25; © Uzhursky/stock.adobe.com, 35; © Vera Kuttelvaserova/stock.adobe.com, 53; © Veronika Ryabova/iStock.com, 55 t., 73 t., 83 t., 96 r., 124 t.; © Viorel Sima/stock.adobe.com, 40, 111 (cat); © Viorika/iStock.com, 90 (cat); © vitalssss/iStock.com, 66 (sushi); © Westhoff/iStock.com, 130 l.; © ysbrandcosijn/iStock.com, 64; © Yuriy Afonkin/stock.adobe.com, 36

With thanks to the cats whose star power shines so brightly in these pages: **MUFASA, RICKY, LUCY,** and **KIFF.**